PRAISE FOR MATT

When Sam Altman introduced me to Matt, he said, 'Matt will add a billion dollars of value to Reddit.' I've been coaching with Matt now for three months, and I think that he already has.

—Steve Huffman, CEO of Reddit

Matt's coaching has brought me clarity, focus, organization, less stress, and higher performance (me and the team). I have always been skeptical of coaches, but I think he can 10x the output of a lot of people, and I hope he does!

—Sam Altman, CEO of OpenAI, former President of Y Combinator

Matt's coaching has changed my life at work and at home. I am able to better name and communicate my emotions, which has allowed me to drive towards underlying interpersonal issues faster and more deeply. I also have been able to have more difficult conversations and get my exec team much more aligned. These may sound like very simple things, but they have been incredibly powerful techniques to drive positive change in a very short period of time.

—Justin Kan, CEO of Atrium

THE TACTICAL GUIDE TO COMPANY BUILDING

MATT MOCHARY

Several sections of this book were written by contributors. They are "Energy Audits and the Challenge of the Technical Founder" in chapter 9, "Exercise" in chapter 10, "Values" in chapter 18, "Titles" in chapter 24, and "Priced Rounds" in chapter 28 by Alex MacCaw, founder and CEO of Clearbit; and "Sales" in chapter 30 by Misha Talavera, co-founder of NeoReach.

Excerpt from *The 15 Commitments of Conscious Leadership* in chapter 15 reprinted with permission from Jim Dethmer, Diana Chapman, and Kaley Warner Klemp.

Editing and design by Indigo: Editing, Design, and More

ISBN: 978-0-578-59928-1
eISBN: 978-0-578-59929-8

CONTENTS

INTRODUCTION

Who am I? Why am I writing this book?

I coach tech startup CEOs (and tech investors) in Silicon Valley, most of whom are young technical founders. As of the writing of this book, they include the CEOs of Coinbase, Plaid, Reddit, Brex, OpenAI, Flexport, Clearbit, Grammarly, Postmates, Atrium, Faire, Front, Newfront, Rippling, and Lambda School.

I earned my bachelor's from Yale and my master's from the Kellogg School of Management in the 1990s, and then joined a private equity firm in Menlo Park (Spectrum Equity). The internet was going nuts, so in 1999 I chose to start my own company called Totality, which maintained private clouds for customers. My co-founders and I raised $130 million and hired 280 people within the first eighteen months. We eventually sold the company to MCI/Verizon, and it is now called Verizon Business.

While I made enough money that I never needed to work again, I realized that Totality was an operational mess. To put it simply, learning how to run a company while running a company is extremely hard. It always seemed like there was just no time.

After the exit, I chose to play (made two movies) and do good (started a foundation to help ex-convicts get and keep legitimate jobs). But I always wondered how I could have improved my performance as a founder. So when I moved back to Silicon Valley to raise my family in 2011, I began studying what I should have done to build a great company. I used the basic three learning methods: reading, talking to subject matter experts, and practicing. And by practicing, I mean the ultimate learning vehicle: teaching.

I started coaching young tech CEOs to see if I could apply the answers in the books to the real world. Amazingly, the solutions worked beautifully.

I noticed that if I described something verbally, CEOs had a hard time creating what I was describing. But if I showed them an example of something, those same CEOs could repeat that example almost perfectly.

So in 2015 I became the "one-day-a-week shadow CEO" at a company called NeoReach. During that one day each week, I held all the company's internal meetings (one-on-ones with each executive, and the executive team meeting). I ran those meetings and was able to show the founding CEO my method. After only a few months, the knowledge transfer was complete. The founding CEO was able to run the meetings (and the system) as well as I could and so took back over.

I have since served as a one-day-a-week shadow CEO at other companies—Brex, OpenAI, Clearbit, Bolt, and AngelList—and will likely continue to do so at others. It's a huge time commitment, but it's a lot of fun.

I now coach both tech CEOs and investors. This is also great fun because I can debunk many of the myths that they believe about one another.

In my coaching, I found several things:

- I repeatedly see the same core issues in nearly every company, and I work with my mentees to address them.
- While there are many books out there with excellent and relevant knowledge for founding CEOs, there is no single book that is a compendium of all the things CEOs need to learn.
- Becoming a great CEO requires training.
- For a founding CEO, there is precious little time to get that training, especially if the company is succeeding.

In this book, I have simply written down the solutions that my mentees and I have come up with. Hopefully it will serve as a compendium so that you can become a great CEO in the very little time you have to do so.

If you are a CEO, new or experienced, this book is meant for you. If you are a first-time CEO, then this book will give you frameworks and answers for your current and future challenges. If you are an experienced CEO, this book will be a good checklist of best-practice benchmarks against which you can rate your company's performance as an organization and your performance individually. In the areas where you discover that you are wanting, the book will give you the target to hit and the tools to implement immediately.

This book is organized into six parts:

1. The Beginning
2. Individual Habits
3. Group Habits

4. Infrastructure
5. Collaboration
6. Processes

"The Beginning" briefly covers how best to start a company and launch a team.

"Individual Habits" covers the most crucial habits to be an effective individual in a company. I'm talking to you, the CEO, but these habits are relevant for everyone, no matter what their position is, so consider modeling them for others to adopt as well. This part discusses organization (getting things done, achieving Inbox Zero), effectiveness (focusing on your top goal, being on time and present, and writing things down), and personal well-being (expressing gratitude and appreciation, doing energy audits, and taking care of your health and well-being).

"Group Habits" covers the most crucial habits to be an effective group, no matter what the group's function or size (including decision-making, impeccable agreements, transparency, conscious leadership, issue identification and conflict resolution, customer empathy, and company culture).

"Infrastructure" covers the tools used to facilitate company effectiveness (the company folder system and wiki, a goal-tracking system, areas of responsibility, no single point of failure, and key performance indicators).

"Collaboration" reviews what a solid organizational structure looks like, as well as techniques to keep an organization working well together (from accountability, coaching, and transparency to meetings and feedback).

"Processes" covers the systems used for each major function of the company (fundraising, recruiting, and sales and marketing).

Additionally, an appendix at the back of the book covers the common question of whether or not to IPO.

All together, these book parts will give you the advice and practical tools you need to lead effectively, provide top-notch products and services to your clients, and be a leader in your industry. With this book, you will tap into the great CEO within.

Matt Mochary
October 2019

PART I
THE BEGINNING

CHAPTER 1: **GETTING STARTED**

There are many reasons to create a company, but only one good one: to deeply understand real customers (living humans!) and their problem, and then solve that problem.

This is explained clearly and thoroughly in *Disciplined Entrepreneurship* by Bill Aulet. I won't repeat or even summarize what he wrote. If you haven't yet launched or achieved more than $1 million of revenue, go read Bill's book first.

CHAPTER 2: **THE TEAM**

In an early-stage company with fewer than twenty people (especially if they are all sitting in one office), good communication and relationships are often easily achieved. This chapter looks at the roles in that early team and reasons why operating can seem so easy at first. Enjoy it while it's there, and be aware that as you grow beyond seventy people and are office operating, changes will be necessary. We'll take a deeper look at scaling up in part IV, but for now let's define best practices for the early team.

CO-FOUNDERS

Starting a company is hard. There are long hours, the constant fear of failing, and many rejections, among other challenges. This burden is further intensified if you try to do it alone. Solo founders have high rates of burnout. The emotional burden is just too high. As with any trend, there are exceptions. But the rule generally holds.

Y Combinator has a strong bias toward accepting co-founder teams (versus solo founders) for this reason. Owning much of something is better than owning 100 percent of nothing. Find a partner, someone who has complementary skills to yours. Share the emotional burden with them. That will ease the load significantly. Give up a large percentage of the company. It's worth it.

Your partner's purpose is not to be value-add forever. As your company grows, you will likely find people with far greater skills whom you will hire. That's okay. Your co-founder's purpose is to help you achieve success in your march to product-market fit. Once you get there and begin the blitz-scaling process, be pleased if they continue to add value beyond that point.

And when you do find a partner, avoid one cardinal mistake: do not create a 50/50 partnership. While 50/50 sounds ideal, it actually leads to real pain if there is no easy way to break a deadlock. Unanimous decisions are tiresome to create day after day after day. Knowing that one person has the ability to decide actually eases the burden for all involved and leads to far better outcomes.

As Alex MacCaw, founder and CEO of Clearbit, writes, "This is key. Two of my previous companies were destroyed by a 50/50 split."

Peter Reinhardt, CEO and co-founder of the customer data infra-structure company Segment, shares a different perspective: "There are ways to avoid deadlock (e.g., third co-founder with small stake à la Charm), and splitting evenly aside from that has been totally fine in my experience with both Segment and Charm. Over time, vesting, cash investment, or differential compensation is a natural way that ownership can diverge."

In all of this, there is a big exception. If you have done this before, have the majority of skills (technical, social, financial) needed to start a company, and are a masochist, then by all means, begin on your own.

Alex MacCaw says, "The key for me in doing it alone is a strong friend group that supports me."

THE TEAM

While it is critical to have a partner to share the emotional burden of starting a company, each additional team member (co-founder, partner, or employee) adds additional complexity in geometric fashion. Each new member must somehow grok the priorities, vision, and actions of the other team members in order to place their efforts in the same direction. The more team members you have, the geometrically harder it is to share what is currently going on with everyone, as well as have everyone be emotionally bought into the decisions being made. Do not underestimate this cost. It is much larger than most founders think.

Y Combinator has another strong belief: founding teams should never grow beyond six until there is true product-market fit. Product-market fit (PMF) is the milestone of having created a product that customers are finding so much value in that they are willing to both buy it (after their test phase) and recommend it. Metrics that show whether PMF has been achieved include revenue, renewal rates, and Net Promoter Score.

The first goal of the company should be to achieve real PMF, not vanity metrics that fool people inside and outside the company that PMF has been achieved. For a B2B company, know that enterprise customers have budgets just for testing new technology and will buy your product to do just that. This does not mean that you have achieved PMF. For these types of customers, only long-term contracts are an indication that they actually value your product and want to use it. There is no magic metric, but for a B2B company, it's hard to imagine PMF at anything less than $1 million in annual recurring revenue.

Why not grow beyond six team members before reaching PMF? Three main reasons: morale, communication and organization, and speed.

MORALE

Until PMF is achieved, the company must have an appropriate morale to be able to adapt to negative customer feedback and potentially pivot the company. No matter what you say to them, when someone joins a ten-plus-person company, they expect stability. If after six months you launch your first product and customers don't instantly rave about it (which is what will happen), the team will become demoralized. It doesn't matter how many times you've announced beforehand that you're still a startup and the team should be ready for this. They will hear the words but not internalize them.

By contrast, with six or fewer people, the environment feels like a team in battle. Chaos is expected. So when chaos is actually encountered, the team meets it with glee. People who join small teams crave the challenge of new things. They want things to be hard.

COMMUNICATION AND ORGANIZATION

When you are a few people in a room, you all know what each person is working on without having to formally report to one another. This has tremendous value because it allows you all to stay in sync without requiring a formal management system, which would suck up significant time and headspace even if done very efficiently.

Once your team grows large enough to not be able to sit next to one another in one room (i.e., more than twenty in one space or even one remote worker), then suddenly information sharing by osmosis disappears. Now you will need a formal management system to succeed. And that requires overhead (usually one full day per week…for everyone!).

SPEED

You can create features in code about ten times faster when writing "prototype code" versus "industrial code." Prototype code is meant only to create a prototype. It is not meant to handle many users, nor be easily understood by those who didn't write it. Industrial code, by contrast, is meant to be easily debugged as well as handle many users. When you are just a few programmers, then there is no choice but to write prototype code, as you don't have enough coder hours to do anything else.

The reality is that your first product should always be viewed as a prototype. You are using it to gather customer feedback only. And that feedback will inevitably vastly alter what your product is, usually to the point of it becoming a completely different product. So all the effort you put into making this initial code beautiful (i.e., industrial) will likely be wasted. If you are small, there will be no temptation to write beautiful, unnecessary code.

If you are a startup in Silicon Valley and have discovered a large potential market, then you will be able to raise significant capital early. This will allow you to hire many people. Investors may well pressure you to do so in order to "win the race to market share." Resist this pressure. It is misplaced.

Startups don't usually fail because they grow too late. They usually fail because they grow too early (i.e., before they have achieved product-market fit).

Now that we've covered getting started, let's look at the day-to-day habits you can be building to ensure smooth operations.

PART II
INDIVIDUAL HABITS

Great companies are made up of great individual performers who work well together as a team. As CEO, you are both the architect of the culture and the central hub in the wheel of information flow that enables the team to function effectively. Your example inspires your team, and your efficiency determines the efficiency of the team. Therefore, the first thing to optimize is yourself.

The chapters in this part cover the habits and methods I have found to be the most effective for fostering individual productivity.

CHAPTER 3: GETTING THINGS DONE

Everyone needs an organizational system to track goals, priorities, and tasks. The majority of successful CEOs that I know use the system outlined in the book *Getting Things Done: The Art of Stress-Free Productivity* by David Allen. While the book is dense, it is definitely worth reading in its entirety.

The essence of Allen's system is this: Each day, process every single item in your inbox (defined broadly as all inboxes [email, Slack, text] and all to-dos). If the action takes less than two minutes to complete, do it immediately. If not, then write down what the required action is, and place it on one of the following lists:

- **Next Actions:** These are the next tasks on your priority list separated into areas of context.

    - Computer (actions for which you need access to your computer)
    - Calls (phone calls that can be completed when you don't have access to a computer, e.g., when riding in a car)
    - Outside (actions that can only be completed outside, such as errands)
    - Home (actions that can only be completed at home)

    Tasks should be written as single actions (as opposed to broad goals). The key is to not have to think about what needs to be done again once the next action has been written down. The next action should be written so clearly that all you need to do is follow its direction when you read it next. Here are some examples:

    Computer
    Write first draft of ten-year company vision and three-month roadmap
    Write first draft of sales playbook

    Calls
    John (650) 555-3452 schedule company off-site

Mary (415) 555-1234 review draft financing docs, paragraph by
paragraph

Outside
Walgreens - pick up prescription

Home
Clean out garage

- **Waiting For:** This is the list of things that you have asked others to
  do and are waiting for them to complete. List the person to whom
  you have delegated a task, the requested action, and the date on which
  you made the request. You can then easily scan your Waiting For list
  and see which aging requests are still outstanding. Move these aging
  requests to your Next Actions list, and ask the person again for the item.

  Waiting For
  Sarah - feedback on sales playbook, 3-18
  Jim - write up issue for next leadership team meeting, 3-19
  Bill - time to meet, 3-19

- **Someday/Maybe:** This is the list of things that you one day want to
  do but don't need to get done now.

  Someday/Maybe
  Schedule a guitar lesson
  Order the book *Getting Things Done* by David Allen

- **Agenda:** Inefficient leaders waste a lot of time reaching out about or re-
  sponding to one-off issues in real time. A much more efficient method
  is to batch your issues and discuss them all at once. This does not apply
  for urgent issues. Those need to be addressed immediately. But by addressing many issues on a regular basis, urgent issues will soon disappear.

  To do this, create and use an Agenda list. This is your list of regular meetings. When you think of something that you want to discuss
  with someone whom you meet with regularly, write it down on your

Agenda list. Then, when you meet with that person, check your Agenda list and review everything accumulated there.

Leadership Team
Are we having enough fun?
Ten-year company vision
Three-month company roadmap

Spouse
What should we do for our winter holiday?
Connect - listen to each other's day for ten minutes each

- **Projects:** This list is for projects that have more than one next action that can only be done one after the other (serially). Write out all the next actions required to get to completion. Then simply add them chronologically to your Next Actions list as the previous action is completed.

- **Goals:** This list is not part of Allen's *Getting Things Done* (GTD) system, but I use it and find it very helpful. Later in the book, I recommend that you create your ten-year company vision and quarterly objectives and key results (OKRs), as well as department, team, and individual quarterly OKRs. I keep a copy of this vision and these OKRs on the Goals list. I refer to it regularly to flesh out my Next Actions list.

- **Review:** This is your pace for reviewing the lists above.

    Daily: Next Actions, Waiting For, and Goals
    Weekly: Someday/Maybe, Agenda, and Projects

Use your calendar to schedule next actions that need to happen on a certain day or at a certain time. I also recommend that you put the above reviews in your calendar. Daily reviews are typically five minutes, and weekly reviews are about fifteen minutes.

There are many tools that will help you maintain a GTD system, from the simple (Evernote) to the potent (OmniFocus). Choose one that fits your level of willingness to learn new functionality.

CHAPTER 4: INBOX ZERO

We all get deluged on a daily basis with inbox messages from email, text, Slack, CRMs, and other online tools. It's critical to have a thoughtful methodology for dealing with them all; otherwise, you'll be buried in communications, and you'll risk missing time-sensitive messages.

Think of your combined inboxes as a single triage room at a hospital. Some cases that come in are urgent, others not so much. It is critical to notice the urgent cases immediately and get them in to see a doctor now. To do so, you must keep the triage room clear. If you use the triage room also as a waiting room, then a new patient can enter the room, sit down in a chair, and bleed out from his stab wound before you even realize he is there. For this reason, every well-functioning hospital separates its triage room from its waiting room and keeps the triage room absolutely clear. To be efficient, you must do the same with your inbox. This means addressing all the urgent cases right away and maintaining Inbox Zero every day.

If you check your email incessantly, multiple times an hour, you are wasting hours of productivity. Instead, batch your time and clean out your entire inbox at those times. I recommend checking your inbox only twice a day (once in the morning, once in the afternoon). Each time, follow this process:

1. If the email takes less than two minutes to address, do it immediately.
2. If it takes more than two minutes, write down a next action for it (according to the steps in chapter 3), and then place the email in its correct location (Next Actions, Waiting For, Someday/Maybe, or Reference). The best way that I have found to do this when using Gmail is to implement the method described in Andreas Klinger's blog post "Don't Drown in Email! How to Use Gmail More Efficiently." Andreas explains how to use Gmail's Multiple Inbox feature to create an inbox for Next Actions, Waiting For, Someday/Maybe, and Reference. You can set the system up in fifteen minutes.

Repeat until you get to Inbox Zero. If you are truly fearless, you can get to Inbox Zero within the hour (yes, even if you have thousands of emails in your inbox right now).

In startups, fires never cease to burn. One of the most common complaints I hear from CEOs is that on a day-to-day basis, they seem to have infinite things to do, yet weeks will go by and they don't feel like they have accomplished anything. This is the result of getting bogged down with the small, immediate things and losing track of the important, long-term ones.

The top goal framework will help you fix this. Greg McKeown, who wrote a phenomenal book on productivity called *Essentialism: The Disciplined Pursuit of Less*, boils this down to one key concept: Schedule two hours each day (i.e., put an event in your calendar) to work on your top goal only. And do this every single workday. Period.

The earlier in the day you schedule this top goal time, the better, so as to avoid other issues (and people) from pressing for your attention. Research shows that we have more decision-making and thought-processing energy early in the day when our brain is freshly rested. Take advantage of this high-quality brain functioning by doing the important stuff first.

During this top goal time, do not respond to emails, texts, calls, and messages. Only work on your top priority (your top goal for the current quarter) during these two hours. If you follow this pattern each workday, you will achieve amazing things.

If you have never scheduled this kind of focused work time, starting off with two hours a day will likely be too great of a leap. Instead, start by scheduling thirty minutes for tomorrow early in the day. If that goes well, then schedule thirty minutes each weekday morning for a week. If that goes well, increase the daily scheduled time to one hour. Continue increasing each week until you find the right balance, knowing that the recommended target is two hours. And if this practice doesn't work for you (i.e., if you already have a very open calendar and are able to get all your priority actions done), then, of course, don't continue scheduling top goal time.

CHAPTER 6: **ON TIME AND PRESENT**

It is critical to be on time for every appointment that you have made or to let the others involved in the meeting know that you will be late as soon as you realize it. This is common decency, yes, but it has a greater importance.

There is someone else on the other side of your agreement to start the meeting at a certain time. They have stopped what they are working on to attend the meeting on time. If you do not show up on time, they cannot start the meeting, but they also cannot leave because they don't know if you'll show up the next minute or not.

Each minute that they are away from their work is a minute of productivity that you have stolen from them. This is not only disrespectful but also counterproductive. If they are a customer, an investor, or a recruit, they will not engage with your company. If they report to you, they will keep quiet but resent you. There is no winning scenario when you waste someone's time.

But life happens. A previous call or meeting may run late. Traffic doesn't always cooperate. Even with careful planning, it's not possible to be on time for every meeting. The good news is that you don't need to be.

It is only critical to let the other members of the meeting know that you will be late as soon as you realize that you will be. And you must come to this realization (and let the other attendees know through whatever channel will get to them the fastest: text, Slack) before the meeting starts. Ideally you'd let them know about the delay before they have to break away from whatever they were doing before the meeting.

In addition to being on time, you must also be present. Being present means that you are composed, prepared, and focused on the subject matter. It can take a few minutes to "get present"—prepare for the meeting, research the topic and the attendees, go to the bathroom between back-to-back meetings, get a drink or snack, and so on. Therefore, I recommend that you plan to arrive to an outside meeting fifteen minutes before it is scheduled to begin. For a meeting in your office, wrap up your current project or previous meeting five to ten minutes before the scheduled time for the next meeting.

To make this easy, I recommend scheduling twenty-five- and fifty-minute meetings only (Google Calendar even has an automated setting for this). This will give you five minutes each half hour and ten minutes each hour to maintain yourself.

When in meetings, I often see CEOs making the mistake of constantly checking their messages. They cannot get away from being "on," if even for a second. This is not only disrespectful but also defeats the purpose of the meeting, which is collaboration with the attendees present. It sends a message that the meeting's content is relatively unimportant. Furthermore, it also breeds a bad habit for the entire company—one that will be hard, if not impossible, to break down the line.

During every meeting, leave your phone in your pocket or facedown. Sticking with the strategies in chapter 3, "Getting Things Done," will help you focus on your meetings and make the most out of your assembled—and expensive—talent. And if the meeting is not efficient, then make it so (see the RAPID method in chapter 12, "Decision-Making").

CHAPTER 7: **WHEN YOU SAY IT TWICE, WRITE IT DOWN**

Whenever you find yourself saying something for a second time (to a second audience or in a second situation), it is highly likely that you will end up saying it again and again in the future. To vastly improve the quality of the communication and reduce the amount of time that you spend communicating the information, *write it down*.

Then, the next time you need to communicate that message, you can simply share it in written form. If it is something that all members of the team should know and remember, put it in a company-wide wiki (see chapter 19). If it is truly seminal to the organization, post it on a wall for all to see.

Alex MacCaw, founder and CEO of Clearbit, says, "Once you see this system working for yourself, start encouraging others in your company to do likewise. Every time you see a question answered on Slack, for example, prompt the questioner to document the response in your company wiki."

CHAPTER 8: GRATITUDE AND APPRECIATION

Confirmation bias is the phenomenon that whatever belief we start out with, we will discover evidence to support it. A corollary to this is that whatever question we ask, we will focus on the answer.

In any situation, we can ask ourselves, "What is wrong here?" or "What is right here?" From an early age, we have been taught by our parents, teachers, and employers to ask the former question. They cannot be faulted. They had the best intentions. In the earliest years of our lives, they were trying to keep us alive. Unfortunately an unintended consequence is that we learned to focus on the negative, and so we continually see the negative. This leads to objectively very successful people being not fully satisfied with their lives, themselves, and so on. If that is where it ended, I wouldn't touch it, as this book is about becoming a great CEO, not about maximizing a feeling of fulfillment. However, that is not where it ends.

It turns out that we perform our best when we are having fun and feeling good about ourselves.

If you want proof of this, go to any kids' sports event where you know the names of the kids. Start cheering positively for the team that is losing, with specific compliments to specific kids: "Great pass, Jimmy." "Way to be in position, George." When a kid takes a shot but misses: "Good idea, Joey, it was the right thing to do." Within five to ten minutes, the tide of the game will start to change toward the team that you are giving specific compliments to. (I have done this many times. And it has worked every time!)

If you are not a parent or don't have access to kid sports, you can try the same technique at the adult sports games that you or someone you know participates in. It works just as well (actually often better) with adults.

So how do we take advantage of this knowledge to generate a good feeling in ourselves? We ask the right question: "What is good about this situation?" "What is good about this team member?" "What is good about my company?" "What is good about my life?" Or we simply fill in the overarching statement "I am grateful for _____." Be as specific as possible: names of people, actions they did, and so on.

I recommend making this a daily practice. I do it first thing every morning. To remember to do it, create a trigger for yourself. A trigger is something that you will see at the time that you want to do the action. Using a trigger allows you to easily create a habit. The easiest trigger, in this case, is a piece of paper with the word *gratitude* printed on it and taped to your night table, the wall by your bed, or the mirror in your bathroom. When you see it each morning, you say the phrase "I am grateful for _____" five times with a different ending each time. (You don't have to say it out loud; you can say it silently to yourself.) The key is to be as specific as possible when you declare what you are grateful for.

Another way to make this a regular habit is to use a journal like Intelligent Change's *Five-Minute Journal*. Keeping the book by your bedside is itself the trigger, as you will see it when you wake up and just before you go to sleep.

If you do this gratitude practice regularly (don't worry if you miss days here and there), your view of your life and yourself will begin to change for the better. And soon afterward you will begin to perform better in life as well, just like the kids on the sports field.

For the cynics out there, being grateful doesn't mean that you will suddenly ignore all the areas of your life or your company that could use improvement. Just the opposite. It only means that you will bring an attitude of joy, as opposed to desperation, when addressing those areas.

Life and company building don't have to be hard or painful. Daily gratitude helps us realize that.

Appreciation is simply an outward extension of gratitude. In gratitude, you speak to yourself. In appreciation, you speak to others. The content is the same.

When you catch yourself feeling grateful about someone or something that they have done, let them know. When you hear something nice said about someone, let them know.

The benefits of this practice are threefold:

- The recipient will feel better about themselves. And we now know what happens when people feel better about themselves.
- The recipient will feel connected and appreciative to you for having brought them this good feeling.
- You will start to view the recipient more positively, since you are now focusing on a positive aspect about them.

In a *First Round Review* article titled "How to Become Insanely Well-Connected," Chris Fralic of First Round Capital says that he reserves one hour each week for follow-ups and outreach, most of which include appreciations. I recommend that you do the same.

Just as with gratitude, giving appreciation should be as specific as possible, as in this example: "John, I appreciate you for writing down our sales process and adding it to the wiki. Thank you."

And when receiving appreciation, there is only one correct response: "Thank you." Do not feign humility by downplaying the act with statements like "It was nothing, anyone could have done it." No. The person is trying to make you feel appreciated. Anything other than "thank you" will rob them of their goal.

CHAPTER 9: ENERGY AUDIT

It is important to maximize your energy. You perform best when you are doing things that energize you. Your goal should be to spend most of your time (75–80 percent) doing things that energize you. If you do, magic will occur.

Get two highlighters, pens, or pencils of different colors (red and green are ideal, but any will do). Print out the last week of your calendar when you were working. Go through each workday hour by hour and ask yourself, "Did that activity give me energy or drain my energy?" Highlight in green those that gave you energy, and highlight in red those that drained your energy. There are no neutrals; every hour must be marked one color or the other.

When finished, look for patterns of where and how your energy is drained. Now think of ways to outsource or eliminate those activities.

Keep doing this energy audit each month until 75 percent or more of your time is spent doing things that give you energy. If you do, you will be able to achieve far more in less time because you will perform far better. You will be in your Zone of Genius.

What is the Zone of Genius? Well, there are four zones:

- Zone of Incompetence
- Zone of Competence
- Zone of Excellence
- Zone of Genius

Tasks in the Zone of Incompetence are the things that other people probably do better than you (e.g., fix your car), and therefore you should outsource if they don't give you joy.

Tasks in the Zone of Competence are the things that you do just fine, but others are as good as you (e.g., clean your bathroom), and therefore you should outsource if they don't give you joy.

Tasks in the Zone of Excellence are the things that you are excellent at (i.e., better than others) but don't love doing. This is the danger zone. Many people will want you to keep doing these things (because they gain significant value from you doing them), but this is the area that you should also look to move away from. This is the hard one!

Finally, tasks in the Zone of Genius are the things that you are uniquely good at in the world and that you love to do (so much so that time and space seem to disappear when you do them). This is where you can add most value to the world and yourself. This is where you should be driving toward spending most, if not all, of your time.

Some people worry that if each of us operates solely in our Zone of Genius then no one will be available to do the un-fun stuff. This is a false fear. There are many personality types. For every activity that feels un-fun to you, there is someone out there who not only excels at it but also loves it (yes, even the "horrible" tasks, like firing people). The key in any organization is for people to be transparent about what their Zone of Genius is, and then map all activities to the right people through an areas of responsibility list (see chapter 21).

Energy audits are the single most powerful tool I know for creating joy and engagement in the workplace. They are meant to be an ongoing practice, not a one-shot action. Continue doing them until the results are mostly green. And then do them once a quarter as a spot check.

ENERGY AUDITS AND THE CHALLENGE OF THE TECHNICAL FOUNDER

BY ALEX MACCAW, FOUNDER AND CEO OF CLEARBIT

Many software companies are started by software engineers. Software engineers are generally smart, are able to figure out and hack systems, and most important, can build version one of their ideas. Unfortunately there is a flip side to this: many software engineers struggle with the transition into full-time CEO. I am one of those engineers. While I can only speak to my experience, I've observed many of the same struggles in my peers.

EMBRACING SALES

In the world of B2B software, sales and customer success will be core aspects of your business. Personally, I've never been a natural salesperson. Indeed, in the past I mostly saw sales as a sign of inefficiency. For someone with an engineering mind-set, verbal communication is lossy and has high latency. Add to that the commission that the average sales rep requires and the bro culture that often accompanies the role, and one starts wishing it could be automated away.

And that's exactly what I tried at first. I kept the sales team at an absolute minimum and automated as much as possible to try to make self-service work. But what I found was that at about $2 million in annual recurring revenue, our growth rate flattened out. So what went wrong?

It turns out I had seriously underestimated two things: sales is critical to gaining trust, and customer success is critical to overcoming technical hurdles.

Trust dissipation is correlated with geographical distance. Humans are hardwired to trust their close friends the most, their immediate peers next, the people they meet in person after that, and the people they meet via videoconference last. By the time they're meeting people over an email exchange, trust is a real issue to making a sale.

Now this might not be a problem if your product sells for ninety-nine dollars a month. The amount of trust you need to make a sale scales with the price, and at that low price level, people are prepared to make a gamble. However, to build a meaningful business, you're going to need a hell of a lot of customers at that price point. And if you're targeting businesses rather than consumers, you'll find there just aren't enough of them to build meaningful revenue in your market. Since businesses are more price insensitive, it makes sense to raise the price of your product to, say, $20,000 a year. But now you have a trust problem.

Enter a competent sales rep. They will smooth the way during the sales process. They will find the key decision maker, make sure that person is listened to, and build trust. They will make promises about the functions of your product, and your customer will always have someone to yell at if things go south.

If your company is like 99 percent of SaaS businesses, you'll find that self-service doesn't work. If we had relied on it, our revenue would have flattened and never recovered. As soon as we added a sales team, our revenue rocketed. Sales might not be the most efficient thing in the world, but it works. And it will continue to work as long as humans are the ones doing the buying. The good news is that sales is incredibly tried and tested; there are many books, tools, and successful examples you can use to pave the way. Don't just respect sales, embrace it.

Now you may be thinking, "That's all well and good. I can see the value in sales, but I kinda suck at it." Well, I'm in exactly the same boat; I would much prefer doing what I do best: talking to computers, not humans. My suggestion, in this case, is that you find an excellent partner in crime to run the go-to-market side of your business. They don't necessary need to be a co-founder, but they need to be someone you trust and someone who can bridge the gap between your company and your customers. Over time you will learn from them and master sales yourself.

In my experience, the best person for this role has high EQ, medium technical understanding, and a fantastic work ethic. I've found a good indicator of their ability is if they understand (or can quickly learn) SQL.

THE TECHNICAL CHASM

The biggest thing I overestimated was the average person's technical literacy. My early team was highly technical people. Surely my customers were technical too?

Unfortunately that couldn't be further from the truth. What I've learned is that the vast majority of people are struggling for air and barely staying afloat in the face of technological changes. Every time they're asked to learn some new tool or concept, they sigh and think to themselves, "Not again. I just finished learning the last thing." It's an uphill battle, but a battle you must fight if you want your customers to be successful.

So what's the best way of addressing this? Is it making your product simpler, improving your help docs, or streamlining your onboarding process? All those things are important, but the only real answer I've found to this problem is customer success. You need dedicated support agents who will hand-hold your customers through the onboarding process, answer questions along the way, and be on hand for any technical issues that crop up.

Again you might be thinking, "But this is highly inefficient. There's no way to automate this process, and I'm going to end up hiring tons of people." You'd be right—it is inefficient, and there is a lot of overhead. You'll need to invest in finding and training these customer success reps, and training them will be a struggle, since in order to communicate with your customers, they will often need to be of the same ilk and technical competence as them. But the alternative is far worse: churn. Your customers are never onboarded or trained properly, they never see value, they end up resenting you and your product, and by the time the renewal comes around, it's too late—their mind is made up.

LEAVING ENGINEERING

I almost think that it's easier for founders with less technical ability to become great CEOs. They build version one of the product, hire engineers, realize they are quickly out of their depth technically, and focus on acquiring the skills needed to become a great CEO.

On the other hand, founders with a deep love of programming often struggle to focus on other areas of the business. Programming defines them; it's what they've been doing since they were teenagers, it's why they got into this business, and it has been part of every day of their working lives.

I'm in the latter camp, and leaving full-time engineering has been a huge struggle for me. If this is something you have no compunction with giving up, then you can happily skip this section, but otherwise, I have a few suggestions.

Sure, you can hire competent people to fill in your weaknesses, and you should absolutely do that, but deep down you know that at some stage you need to make the decision to delegate your engineering and focus on more critical aspects of the business (like hiring). Knowing you're being selfish and focusing on something you love rather than working on something that best serves the business can cause a crippling self-hatred.

I can only say what has worked for me, but this is the process I recommend. It is based on company size:

At zero to fifteen people, I wouldn't worry about this dilemma, just stay heads down coding and building product.

At fifteen to twenty people, you need to start the process of delegating your engineering responsibilities. The only way you're going to achieve this is to absolutely trust your engineering team. Hire the best chief technology officer you can find and the best engineers you can find. At first, review all their code and don't hesitate to bring it in line with your standards. Then, over time, delegate more and more of the engineering.

At twenty to thirty people, most of your work is delegated. At this point, your engineering team has won over your trust, and while you may still think you're the fastest engineer, you see the benefit of scaling yourself outweighs that. The struggle now is giving up the actual programming. It's something you love—of course this is going to be difficult. I wouldn't go cold turkey; I would slowly phase it out to the point where you're coding only one day a week. Then it's crucial you fill in all this free time you now have with a different focus: company building.

This will only work if you embrace and learn to love company building. Finding joy in career development, making that key hire, and putting structures in place so that people love their jobs—these are all things that you must learn to revel in and love. And this will take time, but if your heart's in it, it's all achievable. And if your heart's not in it, think about hiring another CEO.

CHAPTER 10: HEALTH AND WELL-BEING

Building a company will take a physical and mental toll. All the work you put toward your company will be for naught if it costs you your health. It is incredibly important that you focus on both your physical and mental health, and take active measures to improve them.

PHYSICAL AND MENTAL FITNESS

BY ALEX MACCAW

EXERCISE

Ideally, take some form of exercise every day, but at least ensure that you're working out multiple days a week. Figure out what exercise works for you, be that lifting, running, boxing, or some other physical activity. If you find your self-motivation is slipping, get a buddy to train with, sign up for group activities (e.g., Barry's Bootcamp), or get a trainer. If you can't afford a trainer, get the company to pay for it. Your investors won't mind; your physical health is paramount.

MENTAL HEALTH

Company building takes an emotional toll too. It is important that you have someone to speak to, listen to you, and help feelings flow through you. The alternative is bottling up anger, sadness, and fear until you and your company self-destruct. Build a CEO support group composed of your peers. Learn to be vulnerable in front of the company, and practice conscious leadership (chapter 15). Get a therapist; even if you think you don't need one, you will invariably find it useful.

Meditation is also a tool to help focus and quiet the mind. A good company perk is to buy a team account for a meditation app like Calm (calm.com) or Headspace (headspace.com) and then set aside a room in your office for meditating. Put an event in your calendar every day to remind you to meditate, and talk about meditation openly with the company to lead by example.

SLEEP

Many CEOs that I coach find that they sleep far less now than they did before they were running a company. For some, that means waking up in the middle of the night thinking about an issue or a to-do. For others, that means going to sleep late (to finish emails, etc.) and then being woken up by the alarm clock to make it to their first meeting. Either way, the elusive "full night of sleep" becomes a distant memory. These CEOs feel that their bodies are wearing down, and soon they will break in some way.

If this is happening to you, here are the important things to know:

1. This is totally normal! There is nothing wrong with you.
2. Your body is very resilient. It will not break so easily. (I regularly get somewhere between three and six hours of sleep each night, and I am fine.)
3. Your body goes through a sleep cycle of light sleep, deep REM sleep, and lighter sleep again. These cycles usually last an hour and a half each. What makes us feel tired and groggy is being suddenly woken from deep sleep, and this almost only happens due to an alarm clock. Curiously, we feel better rested with six hours of sleep (waking while we are ending a sleep cycle) than we do sleeping for seven hours and having an alarm wake us out of REM sleep. To test this phenomenon, download an app like Sleep Cycle and use it to both track your sleep patterns and wake during light sleep. If nothing else, you will realize that what you are experiencing is common and not abnormal.
4. If you are waking with a thought about an issue or a to-do, it is because your mind is desperately trying not to forget this urgent task. Take these steps to easily quiet your mind:
   a. Keep a notepad by your bed. Write down whatever it is that you woke up thinking about. In the morning, transfer it to your GTD system.

b. Faithfully follow your GTD system during the day. Write down all of your next actions, waiting-fors, and so on. Your mind then will not need to remember these tasks or issues at night, knowing that you have already recorded them in your GTD system.

5. When you do wake during the night, don't fight it. Allow yourself to do productive work. If you aren't motivated to do productive work, do something soothing, like reading from a paper book. Avoid doing something unproductive and stimulating (e.g., viewing social media on a screen). Screens emit blue light that are akin to sunlight and turn the body's circadian rhythm receptors to "wake" mode. Therefore, do not turn to a screen in the middle of the night if you can avoid it. Enable the habit of no screens at night by not allowing your phone or computer to even enter your bedroom.

6. Experiment with your sleeping setup. Throw money at the problem. Here are some things that have worked for others to create a soothing sleeping environment:

   a. Sleep position
      i. Facedown with one leg raised at a ninety-degree angle (as recommended by Tim Ferriss)
      ii. On the side, with a thick pillow between the legs, a thick pillow that elevates the head until the spine is straight, and a thick pillow to hug, all on a memory foam bed

   b. Sleep surface
      i. Memory foam bed
      ii. Biomat

   c. The room
      i. Black-out shades
      ii. White noise machine or soothing music
      iii. No phone or screens in the bedroom (experiment with turning off your Wi-Fi at night)

   d. Rituals
      i. Meditate for several minutes just before going to bed (or in bed).
      ii. Write in your journal.

Many business leaders nod along about how important physical and mental health are to successfully running a business but don't really put it into practice. They find excuses about lacking the time or needing to deal with such-and-such extreme situation before they can think about prioritizing their health again, but the cycle repeats over and over.

Don't fall into this trap. Prioritize your health now. Schedule exercise and meditation on your calendar. Follow a bedtime routine. The more stable your health, the more stable your business will be.

CHAPTER 11: **FINANCIAL HEALTH**

While your business's financial department is managing the company's fiscal health, you'll have to manage your own wealth, especially as it begins to grow with your company's success. Important topics to consider are liquidity, banks versus brokerage firms, and investments.

LIQUIDITY

If your company truly succeeds, you will likely find yourself equity rich but still cash poor. It is important to create liquidity and diversify out of your company's stock. The general rule of thumb is that you should have no more than 25 percent of your net worth in "alternative assets" (illiquid assets). Because your company's equity is likely the majority of your net worth, your net worth is likely more than 95 percent alternative assets. It will be close to impossible to sell 75 percent of your stake in your company. Instead, know that there are two absolute numbers that are significant: $10 million and $100 million.

Most people at $10 million of liquid net worth have the feeling of safety. They breathe a sigh of relief. They are no longer at risk. However, once they sit with that number for a while (and start to raise a family), their mind begins to play through disaster scenarios of how that net worth could disappear completely. Once their liquid net worth grows past $100 million, the catastrophe scenarios dry up and a sense of abundance follows. This is what you are driving for.

The reality is that $10 million is more than enough to live a wonderful life. But give the mind what it wants. After $100 million, each additional dollar will likely not add in any way to your life but may well create a burden (if you buy assets that need to be maintained and supervised).

Therefore, as soon as your company's equity begins to have significant value, start to sell secondary shares until you have sold $10–100 million.

BANKS VERSUS BROKERAGE FIRMS

The next question becomes, "Where do I put the $10–100 million?"

You have three choices:

- Commercial bank (e.g., Citibank)
- Investment bank (e.g., Goldman Sachs)
- Brokerage (e.g., Schwab, Fidelity)

Commercial banks will hold your money and then lend it out to others. The bank gets all the upside of these loans, and you bear all the risk. If the economy tanks and the loans go bad en masse, then the bank fails and (barring a federal intervention) all your assets go to pay off the creditors of the bank itself. Holding your money in a commercial bank is a terrible idea.

Investment banks are similar to commercial banks in that they will use your money to generate profits on their own account. The only difference is that investment banks are not restricted to loans. They can make any kind of bet or investment with your assets. The bank receives all the upside, while you bear all the risk. Again, it's a terrible idea to hold your money at an investment bank.

Finally, there are brokerage firms. These firms do not make loans or investments on their own account. Whatever assets you place at a brokerage firm remain in your name, they are invested only in the way that you direct, and you remain the sole beneficiary. That being said, a brokerage firm is still a business and can go bankrupt if its expenses exceed its revenues for a long period of time (though this is much less likely than at a bank that is almost sure to go bankrupt in a sharp economic downturn). In that case, your assets do get tied up in bankruptcy court, with one exception: US Treasuries. US Treasuries are never held in custody. They are always held for the beneficial owner. If the brokerage firm were to go bankrupt, your US Treasury certificates would be sent directly to you and not be held by the bankruptcy court.

So start by placing your liquid assets in a brokerage firm. Then invest all the cash into US Treasuries while you decide on your investment strategy.

INVESTING

Now that the money is in a safe place, how do you invest it?

David F. Swensen is the chief investment officer for the Yale University Endowment. He is considered the grandfather of portfolio management. He wrote a book specifically for the individual investor titled *Unconventional Success: A Fundamental Approach to Personal Investment.* I consider it the bible for individual asset management. In it, he convincingly describes how professional money managers' ability to create alpha is exceedingly rare, and what few of these managers there are, you likely will never meet them, as they will choose to raise capital only from the most desirable LPs (e.g., Yale University). The money managers you do encounter will likely never create positive net returns for you (after they siphon off their fees and carried interest) when compared to the public equity markets. Therefore, the best approach is for you to simply invest in low-cost index funds (e.g., Vanguard) according to a specific allocation (he recommends about 30 percent US equities, 25 percent non-US equities, 15 percent real estate, and 30 percent US Treasuries) and then rebalance as often as possible.

Unfortunately, rebalancing means putting in lots of trades, and that is painful. Luckily, someone built a tool to solve that problem. Wealthfront (wealthfront.com) is the leading auto-rebalancing investment engine. Many others have copied it, but as of this writing, it is still my preferred vehicle.

PART III
GROUP HABITS

No matter how original and innovative your ideas might be, and no matter how efficient and productive your own habits might be, you won't be able to build a truly exceptional organization alone. Your company's success depends on how well its members work together. Just as individuals develop habits, so do groups. And just as with individuals, it's much easier to start off with good group habits rather than have to change bad group habits down the line.

CHAPTER 12: DECISION-MAKING

The choices you'll face regarding your company will feel endless, from low-impact issues to major ones, and it can be tempting to rush through the decision-making processes. Don't.

CREATING BUY-IN

One of the core challenges in leadership is how to get your team to buy into a decision. It's often easy to make a decision, but it can be much harder to get your team to invest emotionally in that decision. It is important for your team to be invested in a decision; otherwise, their execution will be half-hearted (or won't even happen).

You create buy-in when you make people feel that they are part of the decision and that their input contributes to the final outcome. The more influence they feel they have on the outcome, the more they'll be invested in the final result.

Broadly, there are three ways to make a decision. Each has a different time requirement and creates a different level of buy-in. Unfortunately there are no free lunches here—the method that creates the most buy-in also takes the most time.

The methods to making a decision are as follows:

- Method 1: The manager makes the decision, announces it to the team, and answers questions.
  - Pro: Takes very little time.
  - Cons: Creates very little buy-in from the team. Gets no benefit from the team's collective knowledge and experience.
- Method 2: The manager creates (or assigns someone to create) a written straw man (a hypothetical answer designed to inspire discussion), shares it with the team, invites the team to give feedback (written and verbal), facilitates group discussion, and determines the final answer.
  - Pros: Creates more buy-in. Gets some minimal benefit from the collective wisdom of the team.
  - Con: Takes more time.

- Method 3: The manager invites the team to a meeting where the dilemma is discussed from scratch with no straw man. The manager and the team equally share ideas. The manager acknowledges each idea before making a final decision.
  - Pros: Creates the most buy-in. Gets a lot of benefit from the collective wisdom of the team.
  - Cons: Takes the most time.

Not surprisingly, the greatest benefits require the most work. If you want more buy-in and a better decision, you need to take more time in making the decision.

So which method should you use? It depends on how significant the decision is and how important buy-in is. For everyday, low-impact issues (e.g., the venue for the holiday party), Method 1 is sufficient. For major, core issues (e.g., ten-year company vision), Method 3 is necessary. For everything in between (the vast majority of important decisions), Method 2 is optimal.

There are more tactics involved in successful decision-making and team buy-in than simply choosing the method, though. The three strategies I recommend CEOs consider during decision-making meetings are writing versus talking, the loudest voice in the room, and the RAPID method.

WRITING VERSUS TALKING (ISSUES AND PROPOSED SOLUTIONS)

When two people are discussing an issue, the need to be efficient is important. When a team is discussing an issue, the need to be efficient is paramount because each inefficient minute is multiplied by the number of people in the discussion.

If you're using Method 2 or 3 and want the most effective and efficient decision-making process, require that anyone who wants to discuss an issue write it up, along with the desired solution, ahead of time. The goal of this write-up is to be thorough enough that at the time of the decision meeting, there are few or no questions. This can be achieved in one of two ways:

- The hard way: Write an extraordinarily thorough analysis from the get-go.

- The easy way: Write a draft, circulate it to the meeting participants before the meeting, and invite people to make comments and questions before the meeting. Then write out responses to all of these comments and questions to bring to the meeting.

Jeff Bezos, founder and CEO of Amazon, requires that anyone who wants to bring up an issue or proposal must write up the item fully before the decision meeting (with someone else writing up a counterproposal if necessary). The meeting is then spent reading the write-ups. Once the decision-making team has read them all, a decision is made. If consensus is not reached, the pre-appointed decision maker makes the call. If there are still open questions, then the decision maker assigns one or more people to research and, of course, write the needed follow-up. At the end of the next meeting, the decision is made.

This strategy, though time-consuming for the sponsor, yields extraordinarily thoughtful decisions in a very short amount of time. The extra effort and work by one person creates a net savings in time and energy across the whole group.

That said, imposing this process on a group can be daunting. Here are the steps to ease a group into it:

1. Reserve the first fifteen minutes of the meeting for all participants to write out their updates and issues. Then use another ten minutes of the meeting for all participants to read one another's updates and issues. Then discuss and decide. Use this method for two to three meetings, then...

2. Require that all participants write their updates and issues before the meeting. Do not allow people to bring up an issue that they have not already written up. Use the first ten minutes of the meeting for all participants to read one another's updates and issues. Use this method for one to two meetings, then...

3. Require that all participants write their updates and issues by a certain time before the meeting (e.g., 6:00 p.m. the day before). Require that all participants read and comment on one another's updates and issues before the meeting. People prove that they have read the documents by having their comments in the documents themselves. Do not allow people to make comments in the meeting if they haven't already commented in the documents themselves.

This will make your meetings much more efficient and ensure that meeting time is spent effectively.

The write-up should include both a detailed description of the issue and the proposed solution. Someone may say, "I don't know the answer." It doesn't matter. They should take a guess. Even if they have only 10 percent confidence that their answer is a good one. And they should phrase the proposed solution in very bold, directive terms (e.g., "Do this…"). This may seem aggressive but creates a flag in the sand that generates a much more productive discussion and a quicker decision time, which ultimately is more important than appearing to be humble.

I recommend that all issues and proposed solutions be presented at the weekly team meeting. Allow five minutes of discussion for each proposed solution. If, in that time, consensus is reached, great. The solution is turned into a next action with a directly responsible individual (DRI) and due date.

If not, *do not* spend more time talking about the issue. Instead, turn to the RAPID method (see p. 47).

LOUDEST VOICE IN THE ROOM

(This section was inspired by a conversation with Anthony Ghosn, CEO of Shogun.)

Whenever you choose to use Method 3, remember that in order to get full buy-in, you will have to elicit people's truest thoughts. But as CEO, you will have the "loudest voice in the room." Once people hear your perspective, some percentage will naturally alter their own views to more closely match yours. This percentage is much higher than you might imagine. People assume that, as CEO, you have more information than they do, and therefore your perspective is probably more correct. Later, these same people will not feel fully bought into the outcome because internally they will know that their true thought was not actually heard.

So in order to get the full benefit of your team's knowledge and to make sure that they get to full buy-in, be careful not to tip your hand before all others have shared theirs. The most effective way to do this is to have people write down either their vote or their thoughts before you share your perspective. Or have everyone give a simultaneous thumbs-up or thumbs-down vote.

For an excellent example of this phenomenon and the solution, CJ Reim of Amity Ventures pointed me to *13 Days* by Robert F. Kennedy about the Cuban Missile Crisis, in which President Kennedy kept himself out of the deliberations until each of his advisers was able to form their own viewpoint.

Peter Reinhardt, CEO and co-founder of Segment, says, "Apparently at Amazon they require the most junior people to speak and ask questions first. [This] also becomes a great way to show off junior talent, give more senior folks a chance to observe and give feedback, etc."

RAPID DECISION-MAKING

Emilie Choi, COO at Coinbase, introduced me to a tool developed by Bain & Company to make fully informed decisions with buy-in when

- a team has become too large to easily get all the needed voices in one room, or
- consensus cannot be reached within five minutes of discussion.

It is called RAPID. Here are the steps to this process:

1. Someone identifies an issue or decision that needs to be made. They prepare a write-up with the following details:
   a. The issue
   b. The proposed solution
   c. The list of people needed to make and implement the decision:
      i. R (Recommend): The one who first proposed the issue and solution
      ii. A (Agree): Those people whose input must be incorporated in the decision
      iii. This is usually the legal team, which ensures that no one is breaking the law!
      iv. P (Perform): Those people who will have to enact any decision and therefore should be heard

    v. I (Input): Senior people within the company whose departments and processes will be affected by the decision and therefore should be heard

    vi. D (Decide): The one who will make the decision

        a.) If a decision is irreversible, it should be made by the CEO.

        b.) If a decision is reversible, it should be made by someone other than the CEO.

    d. A section on the document for each person above to write their comments.

2. The R then reaches out to all the As, Ps, and Is to solicit their input. Once their input is received, the document is ready to be reviewed by the D. The R schedules a decision meeting and invites the D, As, Is, and Ps.

    a. If the issue is urgent, the R schedules this decision meeting as soon as it needs to be.

    b. If the issue is not urgent, the R can use the next team meeting as the decision meeting. (This is much more efficient and should be done whenever the issue is not urgent.)

3. At the decision meeting, the D reads through the document. If the D has any questions, the D asks them. If the D's questions can be fully answered in five minutes, the D decides. If the questions cannot be answered in five minutes, the D asks for another round of written responses on the document to answer the D's questions. At the next team meeting, the D reviews these responses and decides.

4. Once the D decides, the D writes up the decision (or asks the R to do so) along with all the next actions (each with a DRI and due date). The D then publishes this decision to the company.

Here is an example:

Timing of Social Events

Reversible or Irreversible Decision: Reversible

Recommend: Matt

Agree: ---
Perform: All
Input: All
Decide: Irene (because it is reversible)

Issue: People who are at the Bench need unbroken time each day to suit up and do experiments from start to finish. In addition, traveling to SF during commuting hours can turn a one-hour trip into a three-hour trip. Social events that are scheduled at 5pm require those from the Bench to depart Sunnyvale at 2pm and lose an enormous amount of productivity.

Proposed solution: Social events to be scheduled at 8pm, until we are together in January.

Erik: I prefer the later time but am open to something in between (6:30pm?).

Katja: I would be fine with it as long as we have a yoga studio close by where I can go in between work and social event :) Also, I like Erik's compromise with starting at 6:30pm.

Raj: :) I am ok with later. 8pm seems ok if it helps the experimental team. Also 6:30 is good.

Marlo: 8pm seems a little late for employees with families. Would we be able to move this time up to maybe 6? I also like the idea of moving team events to the same day as the team meetings.

Katherine: I live in the city, so I'm ok with 8pm. 6:30 works too. If monthly cadence is adopted for moving Thursday meeting to the afternoon, prefer 1st Thursday so it's easy to remember. I also like Thursday meetings being in the morning so that I can get forkable lunch and socialize with the rest of the company I don't see on a daily basis.

Steve: I am ok with either 8 or 5. 6:30 works for me.

Fernando: People who have kids, etc. might not be able to go. The social event will be biased and could negatively impact activities such as recruiting. Suggest polling beforehand to find the best time for the most people. 6:30 is not much better than 5pm. It could be worse coming from the South Bay due to traffic.

Bob: Sounds like a good idea, commuting is a big issue; however, moving it away from the workday may result in less attendance by people with family (especially kids). 6:30 would be good.

Shannon: I also live in the city, so I'm okay with any time. 6:30pm seems good. Or a weekend? Or combining with all-hands meetings.

(Below to be filled out only after all those above already have.)

Irene: Schedule socials in a more central location (although that may be in SF) at a time that works best for everyone. If an earlier time is preferred, then the team events should be planned with enough time in advance (more than one week's notice) such that studies can be planned accordingly. Since I have kids, an evening out where I arrive home after 9 is the same as an evening out starting at 5pm or 8pm.

Victor: No. I usually go to bed early. I also feel this idea could be bad for team members with kids and other family responsibilities.

A proposed solution is to keep after-hours events earlier (such as 5pm) but schedule them only on days where the entire team is already at HQ.

(Below to be filled out only after all those above already have.)

Alice: I agree and think 6–7:30pm is a good idea. Other ideas:

1. Make sure people who are in SF and have families are ok with this.
2. Schedule events far enough in advance to accommodate.
3. (Stealing Matt's idea) Combine social events with days when they will be in office meeting.
4. Schedule social events on a regular cadence (i.e., every third Thursday), which would also help people plan around them.

Bob+1

Decision:

- More than one week's notice to be given on all social events. (Marlo)
- Schedule the social event on the day Bench scientists will be in the office (i.e., Thursdays). (Marlo)
- If needed, 6:30pm (that require travel); if already at HQ, then start at 5pm. (Marlo)
- Establish monthly cadence for socials, once the monthly experimental Thursday team meeting is moved to the afternoon, followed by the social to start at 5pm. (Marlo)
- Marlo and Irene will meet to schedule the upcoming socials for the rest of the year. (Irene)

Victor+1
AZ+1
SS+1
Raj+1
Marlo+1
SV+1
KH+1
Bob+1
KK+1

Once a company starts this process, it is helpful to both track all the RAPIDs that are in process and collect feedback on how to improve the process. For each of these, I recommend a document:

- Create a spreadsheet to track each RAPID that has been created (with a link to the RAPID document), who the R and D are, when the decision meeting will take (or has taken) place, and finally when all the next actions have been completed.
- Create a document for feedback (e.g., what people like or wish would be different) on the RAPID process. After each decision meeting, ask the participants to write in their feedback until the process is working smoothly.

In his 2015 shareholder letter, Amazon's Jeff Bezos introduced us to lightweight, distributed decision-making. He calls irreversible decisions "Type 1" decisions and reversible decisions "Type 2." He goes on to note that "as organizations get larger, there seems to be a tendency to use the heavyweight Type 1 decision-making process on most decisions, including many Type 2 decisions. The end result of this is slowness, unthoughtful risk aversion, failure to experiment sufficiently, and consequently diminished invention."

Each time there is a decision to be made, rate it as irreversible or reversible. If it's reversible, allow one of your reports to be the D (the decision maker in the RAPID process). The decision will be made faster, your report will get the chance to exercise their decision-making muscle, and you will have the chance to gain confidence in your reports' ability to make decisions well.

CHAPTER 13: IMPECCABLE AGREEMENTS

A very common cause of inefficiency in startups is sloppy agreements. People don't show up to meetings on time, and they don't complete the goals that they declare (or they don't declare goals at all). The result is a spreading virus of unproductiveness and decreased morale.

The antidote for this is simple: impeccable agreements. These are (a) precisely defined and (b) fully agreed to (which almost always means written) by all relevant people.

Precisely defined means that a successful follow-through of the agreement can be judged by an objective third party. For example, "expand to Europe" is not precisely defined. An impeccable agreement would be as follows:

Decision: Expand to Europe
Actions:

* Assign five-member advance team to seed the European office, DRI is head of business operations, to be completed by June 1
* Locate office building, DRI is head of operations, to be completed by June 12
* Hire GM Europe, DRI is head of people, to be completed by August 15

The agreement is now precisely defined, with specific actions, DRIs (directly responsible individuals), and due dates.

An impeccable agreement should be written down in a location that is easily accessible by all participants. The only exception is when the agreement is so small, or so regular, that all participants are sure not to forget what the exact agreement is—for example, "It is 12:04 p.m. now. We will start the meeting again at 1:00 p.m. We all agree to be in our seats and present before 1:00 p.m."

As discussed in chapter 6, "On Time and Present," there will, of course, be times when you realize you will not be able to keep an agreement you have made. No problem. As soon as you realize you won't be able to keep the agreement, you let the other members of the agreement circle know.

You also let them know what you *can* do. This gives them the opportunity to adjust and maintain productivity. Here are some examples:

- You agreed to be at the team meeting by 10:00 a.m. But because of unusual traffic, you estimate that you will reach the office at 10:05 a.m. You immediately contact your team and let them know that you will be at the meeting by 10:10 a.m. The other attendees can begin with agenda items that don't require your input.
- You are the vice president of sales, and you agreed to bring in more than three new customers and more than a million dollars in new annual revenue by the end of the quarter. By the end of the second month of the quarter, the pipeline shows only one new customer potentially closing before the quarter ends. You immediately let your CEO know that you are not going to hit this goal, and you tell your CEO what you realistically will be able to do. The CEO can then jump in to help process customer leads to help meet the target.

If, however, you fail to inform the agreement circle, then you have broken that agreement. The other attendees are unable to adjust, and both productivity and morale slip.

There must be consequences for breaking agreements. Implementing these consequences is a two-part process. The first time someone doesn't meet an agreement, you point it out to them immediately. If they apologize, you respond that apologies are not needed, and all that is required is that they only make agreements that they can commit to and that they meet all the agreements they make, whether by adherence or by prompt communication that they need to alter the agreement.

If the person continues to fail at these, there is only one consequence that makes sense: they can no longer be part of the company.

Your team members are smart. When there are problems, they know it. Hiding negative information from them does not make them feel better. If anything, it makes them more anxious.

Just as you don't know if your team members will share negative information with you until they do so for the first time, your team members don't know if you are willing to share negative information with them until you do. Our imaginations are much more powerful than reality.

Share all relevant information with your team, both positive and negative. Here are some examples:

- The good: "We hit $20 million in annual recurring revenue this month."
- The not good: "Our VP of sales is leaving the company. She made tremendous contributions, but I was unable to create an environment that kept her motivated. To correct this going forward, I will be asking for candid feedback from all of my reports in each of my weekly one-on-ones."

This will give the team great comfort and enable them to use their brilliance and talents to adapt.

There are only two pieces of information most companies choose not to share openly: (1) individuals' compensation and (2) individuals' performance reviews (particularly performance improvement plans). Public knowledge of these items often causes heated debates, relative comparisons, and even shame, all of which are big distractions.

However, some companies choose radical transparency, sharing both of these types of information with success. Such complete sharing should only be done if the entire company is trained in radical transparency. One such training comes from the Conscious Leadership Group, of which radical transparency is just one part.

CHAPTER 15: CONSCIOUS LEADERSHIP

Conscious leadership is a system developed by the Conscious Leadership Group as a way of directing your team while being more interested in learning than being right. When our egos make us afraid to be wrong, that fear leads us to defend our ideas at all costs and to work hard to convince others that we are right—often with anger. This works to break a company apart, not build it up. By contrast, conscious leadership is about

- recognizing when these emotions (fear, anger, sadness) have gripped our thought processes; and
- releasing these emotions and shifting back to a state of curiosity where we are receptive to all ideas and creativity, even if they seem to contradict our own. It is in a state of playful curiosity that truly elegant solutions are achieved.

Jim Dethmer, Diana Chapman, and Kaley Warner Klemp explain this concept thoroughly in their book *The 15 Commitments of Conscious Leadership*. The following excerpt provides a good window into the concepts.

LEADING FROM ABOVE THE LINE

At any point, a leader is either above the line or below the line. If you are above it, you are leading consciously, and if you are below it, you are not. Above the line, one is open, curious, and committed to learning. Below the line, one is closed, defensive, and committed to being right.

Many people lead from below the line—it's a common state stemming from millions of years of evolution. As soon as we sense the first whiff of conflict, our lizard brain kicks in. Fear and anger rise up, then we get defensive and double down on being *right*. At this point we're firmly below the line.

Knowing that you're below the line is more important than being below the line. The first mark of conscious leadership is self-awareness and the search for truth. The second is pausing, taking a second, shifting yourself into an open and curious state, and rising above the line.

CONSCIOUS PRINCIPLES

The following are principles to live your life by in order to shift yourself above the line.

TAKING RADICAL RESPONSIBILITY

I commit to taking full responsibility for the circumstances of my life and for my physical, emotional, mental, and spiritual well-being. I commit to supporting others to take full responsibility for their lives.

Taking full responsibility for one's circumstances (physically, emotionally, mentally, and spiritually) is the foundation of true personal and relational transformation. Blame, shame, and guilt all come from toxic fear. Toxic fear drives the victim-villain-hero triangle, which keeps leaders and teams below the line.

Conscious leaders and teams take full responsibility—radical responsibility—instead of placing blame. Radical responsibility means locating the cause and control of our lives in ourselves, not in external events.

Instead of asking "Who's to blame?" conscious leaders ask, "What can we learn and how can we grow from this?" Conscious leaders are open to the possibility that instead of controlling and changing the world, perhaps the world is just right the way it is. This creates huge growth opportunities on a personal and organization level.

LEARNING THROUGH CURIOSITY

I commit to growing in self-awareness. I commit to regarding every interaction as an opportunity to learn. I commit to curiosity as a path to rapid learning.

Self-awareness and learning agility are known to create sustained success in leaders—they form the foundation of conscious leadership.

Conscious leaders are passionately committed to knowing themselves, which is the basis of their willingness to live in a state of curiosity. At any point, leaders are either above the line (open, curious, and committed to learning) or below the line (defensive, closed, and committed to being right).

Being "right" doesn't cause drama, but wanting, proving, and fighting to be "right" does. Even though conscious leaders get defensive like everyone else, they regularly interrupt this natural reactivity by pausing to breathe, accept, and shift.

FEELING ALL FEELINGS

I commit to feeling my feelings all the way through to completion. They come, and I locate them in my body, then move, breathe, and vocalize them so they release all the way through.

Great leaders learn to access all three centers of intelligence: the head, the heart, and the gut.

Resisting and repressing feelings is standard operating procedure in most organizations. Feelings are viewed as negative and a distraction to good decision-making and leadership.

Conscious leaders know that feelings are natural and expressing them is healthy. They know that emotion is energy in motion; feelings are simply physical sensations.

The five primary emotions are anger, fear, sadness, joy, and excitement. Knowing how to express them all of the way through to completion helps us develop emotional intelligence. Each primary emotion has a unique energy pattern and set of sensations in and on the body. Every feeling we experience invites us in a specific way to grow in awareness and knowing. Repressing, denying, or recycling emotions creates physical, psychological, and relationship problems.

To release emotion, first locate the sensation in the body and then vocalize the feeling.

Conscious leaders learn to locate, name, and release their feelings. They know that feelings not only add richness and color to life but are also an essential ally to successful leadership.

SPEAKING CANDIDLY

I commit to saying what is true for me. I commit to being a person to whom others can express themselves with candor.

Leaders and teams have found that seeing reality clearly is essential to being successful. In order to see reality clearly, leaders and organizations need everyone to be truthful and not lie about, or withhold, information. They need candor. Candor is the revealing of all thoughts, feelings, and sensations in an honest, open, and aware way.

Speaking candidly increases the probability that leaders and teams can collectively see reality more clearly. Withholding is refraining from revealing everything to all relevant parties. Withholding also decreases energy in leaders, which often shows up as boredom or lethargy in them and relational disconnection in the team.

Rather than withholding, conscious leaders practice revealing. They reveal not because they are right, but because they wish to be known. Through this transparency, they create connection and open learning. Conscious listening is one of the most important skills for effective leadership: by identifying our listening "filters," we can let go of them and become fully present to the expression of the other person.

Conscious listening takes courage: we must listen for the content (head center), the emotions (heart center), and base desire (gut center) being expressed by the other person. It is best to start with candor in relationships only when you have a shared commitment to it, along with the necessary skills, including being able to speak unarguably.

ELIMINATING GOSSIP

I commit to ending gossip, talking directly to people with whom I have a concern, and encouraging others to talk directly to people with whom they have an issue or concern.

Even though gossip has long been a part of office culture, it is a key indicator of an unhealthy organization and one of the fastest ways to derail motivation and creativity.

Gossip is a statement about another made by someone with negative intent or a statement the speaker would be unwilling to share in exactly the same way if that person were in the room.

Gossip is an attempt to validate the righteousness of a person's thinking and is below the line; it is not a comment designed to serve the person being discussed.

People gossip to gain validation, control others and outcomes, avoid conflict, get attention, feel included, and make themselves right by making others wrong. In short, people usually gossip out of fear. If you gossip, clean it up by revealing your participation in the gossip to everyone involved.

When leaders and teams learn to speak candidly with each other, they benefit from the direct feedback about issues within the organization that otherwise could derail creative energy and productive collaboration.

INTEGRITY

I commit to the masterful practice of integrity, including acknowledging all authentic feelings, expressing the unarguable truth, keeping my agreements, and taking 100% responsibility.

Integrity is the practice of keeping agreements, taking responsibility, revealing authentic feelings, and expressing unarguable truths. It is essential to thriving leaders and organizations.

Conscious leaders are impeccable with their agreements. They make clear agreements, keep them, renegotiate them when needed, and clean them up when broken. Integrity is fundamental to conscious leadership and successful thriving organizations.

GENERATING APPRECIATION

I commit to living in appreciation, fully opening to both receiving and giving appreciation.

Committing to appreciation, along with avoiding entitlement, helps leaders and organizations grow value and connection in the workplace.

Appreciation is comprised of two parts: sensitive awareness and an increase in value.

Entitlement arises when rewards and benefits become an expectation instead of a preference. Living in appreciation has two branches: being open to fully receiving appreciation and being able to fully give appreciation. For most, it is more difficult, and people are more afraid, to receive appreciation than to give it. To avoid receiving appreciation, people strategically deflect it. Masterful appreciation is sincere, unarguable, specific, and succinct.

Appreciation allows the unique gifts in the community to be recognized.

LIVING A LIFE OF PLAY AND REST

I commit to creating a life of play, improvisation, and laughter. I commit to seeing all of life unfold easefully, and effortlessly. I commit to maximizing my energy by honoring rest, renewal, and rhythm.

Creating a life of play, improvisation, and laughter allows life to unfold easily and energy to be maximized. Play is an absorbing, apparently purposeless activity that provides enjoyment and suspends self-consciousness and a sense of time.

It is also self-motivating and makes you want to do it again. An imposed nose-to-the-grindstone culture will lead to higher levels of stress, guilt, employee burnout, and turnover. Energy exerted with this type of "hard work" is wrought with effort and struggle, whereas energy exerted through play is energizing.

Most leaders resist play because they think they will fall behind if they aren't seriously working hard. Organizations that take breaks to rest and play are actually more productive and creative. Energy is maximized when rest, renewal, and personal rhythms are honored.

Conscious leaders who value and encourage an atmosphere of play and joy within themselves and in their organizations create high-functioning, high-achieving cultures.

EXPLORING THE OPPOSITE

I commit to seeing that the opposite of my story is as true as or truer than my original story. I recognize that I interpret the world around me and give my stories meaning.

Conscious leaders practice simple ways to question the beliefs that cause suffering, starting with "Is it true?" and "Can I absolutely know it is true?" The turnaround exercise allows leaders to practice shifting their beliefs from knowing to curiosity. When conscious leaders let go of the righteousness of their beliefs, they open to curiosity and align with their deepest desires.

EMPATHY

Spiritual teacher and author David Deida goes one step beyond recognizing and releasing negative feelings and teaches that empathy is the key to success. To truly feel the feelings of those around you—customers, investors, and team members alike—you must get very curious about their situations and then really imagine yourself in their shoes. If you do this, people will sense it and immediately trust and like you, because they will feel that you care about them and understand their circumstances. They'll trust you to lead them because they know you'll truly consider their interests in your guidance.

JOY VERSUS FEAR

When people start diving into the conscious leadership work, they quickly lose their fear. And just as quickly, they realize that fear was their primary motivator—fear of failure, fear of letting people down. Once fear is gone, their life becomes much better, but their business suffers.

If you find yourself in this situation, keep pushing forward with the conscious leadership work *quickly* to get to a place where you are motivated by joy. Then you will have the best of all worlds. Joy is an even better motivator than fear, so your business will thrive. And your life will be amazing!

CHAPTER 16: ISSUE IDENTIFICATION AND CONFLICT RESOLUTION

Issues and personal conflicts continually exist in your company. The only question is whether you know about them. If you know about them, you have a chance of resolving them.

ISSUE IDENTIFICATION

There are two excellent ways that I know of to encourage people to identify the key issues in the company that need to be solved.

The first: Have each person imagine that they are the CEO and ask themselves the question, "What are the most important issues (maximum three) for me to solve in the next ninety days?" Allowing people to put themselves in the CEO role gives them permission to think like an owner.

The second: Just as people's fullest thoughts about someone can be drawn out by sourcing anger, fear, sadness, joy, and excitement, so too can someone's thoughts about the company.

At every quarterly off-site meeting that I facilitate for team bonding, we do the following exercise:

1. I ask all team members to open a document that only they have access to and write down their thoughts about the company when they source their joy, excitement, sadness, anger, and fear.
2. For their thoughts of anger and fear, each person writes:
   a. Fact. This is what a video camera captured. There is no judgment or opinion here, only physical actions that have occurred that no one would dispute. Keep this short.
   b. Story. These are all the thoughts, opinions, and judgments that you have on the facts above.
   c. Proposed solution. These should be very specific action items with DRIs and due dates.
3. While they are doing that, I create a document with those headings and give access to all.

4. Then I ask everyone to copy and paste their writings (with no attribution) under the correct heading in the group document.
5. We all read the document.
   a. The writings of joy and excitement make us all feel inspired and renew our feeling of group success.
   b. The writings of sadness allow us to feel bonded over shared loss.
   c. The issues and solutions posed in anger and fear give us an issues roadmap to be unpacked and resolved one by one in the weekly leadership meetings over the course of the upcoming quarter.

It is a very simple and effective exercise. I recommend that you do it with everyone in the company on a quarterly basis.

CONFLICT RESOLUTION

Interpersonal conflict arises often. And almost always it is due to people (a) not fully sharing their feelings and thoughts and (b) not feeling heard. There is a laughably simple method for solving this issue. Stephen Covey shared the technique in *The 7 Habits of Highly Effective People: Powerful Lessons in Personal Change*. Marshall B. Rosenberg codified it in *Nonviolent Communication: A Language of Life*. And Chris Voss showed its effectiveness in his excellent *Never Split the Difference: Negotiating as If Your Life Depended on It*. I recommend reading all three of these books to get fully immersed in their techniques, but here is the thousand-foot view.

When people feel distrust or dislike for each other, it is usually because they don't feel heard. For me to respect you, I don't need for you to agree with me. But I do need for you to hear what I have to say. When I tell you my perspective (which I, of course, believe to be right) and you aren't immediately convinced, then I assume that you didn't really hear or understand what I said. If you start sharing your perspective, I will be uncompelled and unwilling to truly listen, because you haven't been willing to consider mine. And the cycle spirals downward to distrust and dislike.

There is a simple fix. I only need to prove to you that I have "heard" you. And to do that, I only need to *repeat back what you've said in summary form* (by saying, "I think I heard you say…") until you say, "That's right!" Then you will feel heard. You will now be open to hearing what I have to say.

Here is an experiment that proves this principle. The next time you encounter a person who is repeating themselves, stop them and ask if you can state back what they've already said. They will say yes. You then summarize what they've said and ask if you got it right. If they say yes again, then watch to see if they continue to repeat themselves. They will not.

For you, as a company leader, to resolve conflict, you only need to get each person to state their deepest, darkest thoughts, and then prove that each has heard what the other has said. This can be done verbally or in writing. I prefer the written method, as it takes about a third of the time, requires almost no facilitation (i.e., it's easy to stay on script), and the action items that come out of it are impeccable agreements.

If you are the facilitator, here's how the written method works. First, get both people in the same room. Have them bring their laptops so they can share their documents with each other at the appropriate times. Then go through the following steps:

Step 1: Ask each person to write down their deepest work-related thoughts about the other person.

You say:

1. Open up a document. Please give me (the facilitator) access, but do not give access to the other person yet. On the document, write five categories:
   a. Anger (present)
   b. Fear (future)
   c. Sadness (past)
   d. Joy (present and past)
   e. Excitement (future)
2. In every major relationship that we have, we have feelings of anger, fear, sadness, joy, and excitement. When you think about the other person and you focus on the anger that you feel, what thoughts come to mind? Please state those thoughts in the following way:
   a. Feeling: Anger

b. Fact: You did or said… (This should be only what a video camera would have seen; no opinion, thought, or judgment.)
c. Story: The thought that I had was…
d. Request: You do or say… (This should be an action that the other person can take to fully address this situation.)

Here is an example:

a. Feeling: Anger
b. Fact: You walked by me the other day and I didn't hear you say hello.
c. Story: The thought that I had was that you purposely ignored me and thus were really saying "screw you!" to me.
d. Request: From now on, when you walk by me, please say hello.

As the facilitator, look at both documents and make sure that they are filled out correctly. Encourage the separation of fact and judgment as much as possible. Make sure they are as specific as possible about the actions the other person did and how it made them feel. Realize that any conclusions drawn from the other person's actions are simply stories in their head, only the feelings one has, and any specific actions are facts.

If one or both are reluctant to say anything, which is often the case, you supply the thoughts that you might have if you were in their shoes. Be dramatic. Become an actor. Get into the role. State the thoughts as explicitly as they would appear in your own mind. Use swear words.

The participants will start to guide you. They are likely to say, "That's close but not quite it. The thoughts I have are more like…" When they slow down or don't seem willing to go further, again state the thoughts for them. Each time you do so, it allows them to go further. Do this until each person has written down their raw, unvarnished thoughts around anger toward the other. Once they get that right, they can usually get through fear, sadness, joy, and excitement on their own.

Now ask each participant to cut and paste the joy and excitement sections to the top of the document. For the person sharing their emotions and thoughts, it is hard to feel joy and excitement until they have first written down their thoughts around anger and fear. But when the recipient reads the document, it is best for them to first see how the sharer actually has positive thoughts about the recipient. This validates the relationship and motivates the recipient to do what is needed to repair that relationship. Therefore, it is important for the recipient to read the thoughts around joy and excitement first.

Step 2: Person A (the person with less power in the relationship) shares access to their document with Person B.

Person B reads Person A's thoughts around joy and excitement about Person B. Person B should simply say "thank you" to Person A after reading these thoughts.

Person B then reads Person A's first thought around anger about Person B. You, the facilitator, then follow this script:

1. Facilitator to Person B: "Do you want to make Person A feel anger and have these thoughts?"
2. Person B: "No."
   a. If the answer is yes, then the two should not be in a relationship together. That means that one will likely need to be let go from the organization. Regardless of seniority, the person to be let go should usually be the person who wants the other to feel anger. That person will likely create toxic relationships with others as well and eventually will have to leave the company anyway.
3. Facilitator to Person A: "What request do you have of Person B?"
4. Person A: "Please do the following:…"
5. If Person B agrees, have Person B write down the action item (with their initials and due date) just below the fact and story of Person A.
   a. The goal here is to cocreate a plan so that misunderstanding and acrimony do not enter the relationship again. Person A goes first. Person B adds their thoughts. They go back and forth until they have agreed on a written plan.
   b. Verbal agreements are not impeccable. We all understand words a little bit differently. To make this agreement impeccable, one of the participants writes down the plan and the other adds their initials and a +1 to note their agreement.
6. Facilitator to Person A: "Do you feel heard? Do you feel that Person B wants to have a positive relationship with you?"

7. Person A: "Yes."
   a. If the answer is no, get curious and find out why. Repeat the steps above again until the answer is yes.
   b. Do not move on to a second anger item yet.

Step 3: Person B shares access to their document with Person A. Repeat the same script as in Step 2.

Now both Person A and Person B have

1. affirmed that they want to be in a positive relationship with each other, and
2. accepted the feedback and created an action item to resolve it.

Step 4: When the "aha" moment of understanding and compassion for each other occurs, seal it with a physical connection: a hug, a handshake, or a high five. If the two have hugged in the past, ask them to do so again now. If the most they have done in the past is shake hands or high five, then ask them to do that now. This physical connection symbolizes the new understanding and puts a capstone on the event.

Step 5: Ask each person for feedback on the process.

What did they like that you (as facilitator) did? What did they wish that you had done differently?

Step 6: Set a meeting for one to two weeks out between Person A, Person B, and the facilitator.

If the first meeting was rocky, then also schedule a one-on-one with each participant before the second group meeting. During these one-on-ones, help each person share their deepest thoughts, stay on script, and view the feedback they receive as a gift.

At the second group meeting, confirm that both Person A and B have completed their action items. This will prove to each other that there is a real desire for a positive relationship.

Do Steps 2–4 on the remainder of the issues identified under anger and fear for each person.

In my experience, when two people who previously felt hatred toward each other have shared their thoughts (and been heard) around all five of the basic emotions they feel toward the other, they create an understanding and respect for each other, even if they still do not agree with the other's positions.

CHAPTER 17: CUSTOMER EMPATHY

Just as it is important to be conscientious when leading your team and to encourage empathy between team members, it's crucial to be conscientious and empathetic for your customers too. But what does that mean in practical terms? Remember that you are not making a product—you are solving a customer problem. It is therefore critical that you continually live that customer problem. Only then can you solve it well. To live the customer problem, you must sit with the customer, ask them about their life, and observe their daily routine, on a regular and constant basis.

If you actively listen to your customers' pain, they will trust you to decide which solution will best erase that pain. Use the phrase "I think I heard you say…" often. This will make the customer feel heard.

If you do not listen to your customers' pain, then they will do the thinking and make demands about what the solutions should be, no matter how impractical. Once those demands are voiced, it's hard to walk them back.

Build trust with your customers quickly by actively listening to their pain. Really imagine what it's like to have their needs and frustrations. Voice what you perceive back to the customer ("It seems that you feel anger when…"). When your customer says, "That's right!" trust will be established. You want this to be a group habit, so teach this methodology to everyone in your company, from sales to engineering.

It is particularly important to instill this mind-set in your engineering department, because the engineering department tends to sit the furthest away from the customer and only hears about the customer in abstract terms. The solution is to have customer support and sales leaders distill feedback and meet with the product team once a month to ensure feedback gets in the next cycle.

Your sales department will already have a customer-centric mind-set, but it is important for them not to prioritize every customer request. Customers know exactly what pain they are feeling, and they know that they want relief. But they don't know how feasible each solution is. You do. After identifying all customer pain points, for each, rate the amount of pain that the customer feels and the degree of difficulty for you to solve it. Then work first on the issues with the highest customer pain that are the easiest for you to solve.

CHAPTER 18: COMPANY CULTURE

Culture is the unspoken set of rules that people in a group follow when interacting with one another. You act differently when you're in a bar than when you're at a family dinner. That's because the rules that run the interactions between the different nodes in the networks have changed. Culture is the name for those rules.

Company culture is important because it affects how team members interact with one another and with customers. There are various ways to build and shape company culture, and the main ones that I tend to focus on are through values, fun, celebration, hours of operation, meals, cross-team communication, and politics minimization.

Values are a critical element in your company's culture, and your company will function at its most efficient if your employees understand and share them. Once your team has a referenceable shared set of values, they can make decisions without you and, more important, evaluate candidates for culture fit. As the team grows, interactions between new hires and the core team, who defined the company's values, diminish. Having a set of established and referenceable values helps disseminate those values to new team members without daily interactions.

One misconception CEOs sometimes have is thinking they get to choose the values. By the time you have thirty or so employees, your company has a set of values whether you like it or not. It's now your job to codify what's already there. While it is possible to change a value, it will take a lot of work.

Agreeing on what your values are is the kind of statement that needs maximum buy-in, so it should involve your whole company. Send out a survey, and gather contributions from everyone. Ask your team to suggest both a value and the name of an employee who exemplifies it. Then arrange all the suggestions into common themes, and have your leadership team vote on the final cut.

Once you have agreed on your values, use them to guide your hiring and firing. Bring in people who want to live by these principles, and let go of people who don't. Otherwise, your values will have no meaning.

Distribute your values, print them out, and repeat them until your team knows them back to front. Every week at the all-hands meeting, highlight a value and a person whose actions best exemplify that value that week.

VALUES

BY ALEX MACCAW

The following examples are some of Clearbit's values. They combine a short, pithy statement (easily rememberable) with a longer description for clarity.

- Care (Give a shit). Empathize with customers. Take the time to understand their frustrations, needs, and desires.
- Craft (Master it). Own your craft. Never stop learning and improving.
- Team (Work together). Teamwork makes the dream work. Fill gaps. There's no such thing as "it's not my job."
- Truth (Say it). Be up front and candid. Say it like it is. Hold yourself and others accountable.
- Initiative (Be resourceful). Don't wait for permission. Figure it out—or figure out who can.
- Fun (Have it). Don't take yourself too seriously—life is short.

FUN

When creating company culture, do not underestimate the value of fun. If people are having fun, they spend more time, energy, and awareness at the company. This leads to better problem-solving and collaboration, which leads to a stronger company that creates more value.

Host events that you enjoy, and then invite (but don't require) your team members to join you. Your litmus test is whether your team members are hanging out with you and one another outside of work. If yes, you are likely creating good culture. If not, increase your efforts to practice conscious leadership (chapter 15) and keep working to create buy-in for your values.

- Take the team out for lunch at a local restaurant.
- If you don't have catering, which has its own serving time, then provide suggested times for lunch so people can eat together (with a calendar event).
- Find fun off-site activities. The local amusement park is just as fun as an extravagant international trip.
- Play team sports like dodgeball and soccer.
- Rent out a local movie theater. (They are almost always available for a morning screening.)

CELEBRATION

Most companies are so focused on improving that they forget to celebrate. But celebration, like fun, is a key to building positive morale. Celebration doesn't mean lavish drunken parties. Quite the opposite. Celebration means taking a moment to appreciate the good that the company has achieved, as well as the good that departments, teams, and individuals have achieved.

Here are some ways to celebrate:

- Publicly acknowledge these achievements at all-hands and team meetings.
  - Remember to celebrate the very necessary but often overlooked teams on the core product.
  - You don't need to celebrate every team at every meeting. Create a rotation.
- Create a standing demo meeting where teams can show off their most recent creations.
  - This should not be a required meeting, but rather should occur over a meal (lunch) or drinks (Friday afternoon).

HOURS OF OPERATION

The question of working hours is inevitable in every company. Should you enforce specific starting and ending times? Total number of hours?

Remember, the key metric is output, not hours. If you impose hours, people often will simply put in the required hours but without effort or enthusiasm, and you'll make little progress. The key is to inspire and motivate your team so that long, hardworking hours are not an imposition but a choice.

If you are creating and tracking goals, habits, agreements, and key performance indicators (see chapter 23); openly receiving and providing feedback (see chapter 27); and creating fun, then people will be naturally motivated to work hard. They'll see where the company is going, how it's moving forward, and how their efforts and their team members' efforts are contributing. They'll know that they are heard, and they'll be having fun.

Furthermore, if your team members are hitting their individual goals and objectives and key results, ask yourself if enforcing set times in the office really matters or if you are just enforcing them for appearances' sake. The same goes for working at home—it's really all about the output rather than the location or time spent working.

Remember to always lead by example. Be the first one to show up each day. Be the last one to leave. Once you have department heads, they should also set this example for their departments. Do not hire department heads who are unwilling to do so.

Whatever your teams' working hours end up being, make sure there is a core period of the day when everybody is available (whether online or in the office). Set a regular meeting (a short stand-up meeting) at the beginning of this core set of hours.

MEALS

Offering meals is a particularly positive benefit. Mealtimes together allow team members to bond organically and with a wide range of people. Having people go out to get their own food usually causes them to stick with the same small subgroup each day.

Offering lunch thus creates a more bonded overall team. Offering breakfast and dinner allows people to easefully extend their workday. Thus, there are benefits to offering meals beyond simply the pretax calculus.

(The pretax calculus is that meals are a commodity. If you provide meals company-wide, then you can deduct the expense as a business expense. If you do not, your team members must use post-tax dollars to buy those meals. Thus, providing meals is a way of providing benefits to your team on a pretax basis.)

Encourage team members to be present at meals so that they interact with one another. This means no electronics (phones or laptops) at the meal table. Encourage the team to meet at the same time each day by creating a shared calendar event. All this will improve team bonding and trust.

CROSS-TEAM COMMUNICATION

As your company grows, you'll find that communication between members of disparate teams slows to a halt. This is especially prevalent between engineers and the rest of the company. This is further amplified if a good portion of your team is remote.

One solution that I've seen work is to randomly assign team members every week to meet, get a coffee, or hang out virtually. There are tools like Donut (donut.com) to facilitate this.

POLITICS MINIMALIZATION

Politics are created when someone successfully lobbies the CEO or their manager for some kind of benefit. Others see this, so they in turn lobby. They then gain benefit, and the virus spreads quickly throughout the organization, all the while directing company energy away from customer problem-solving.

It often begins very innocently: "Excuse me, can I please talk to you about a raise? I have been at this company for a year now and have shown utter dedication by doing such-and-such, and I believe that I now deserve a raise…"

This sounds compelling, and you, of course, want to reward dedication. But if you give a raise based on this conversation, then the whole company will learn that the way to get a raise is to simply ask you for it.

Suddenly everyone will be trying to curry your favor. Be very careful here. You may enjoy this behavior, but it is toxic for the company.

The only way to prevent politics is to never allow lobbying to be successful, and the only way to do this is to have a written policy about as many situations as possible, particularly around compensation, raises, and promotions. Apply this policy to all team members, all the time.

It is difficult to create objective criteria for compensation, raises, and promotions, but there are models. The most successful method I know of is called grade level planning (GLP)—at least, that's what Tesla calls it (another common term is "Levels and Ladders"). It calls for a very detailed definition of every position in the company and every seniority level, along with specific compensation metrics for each position and level. This is then shared throughout the company. Team members can then clearly see what they need to do to receive the next compensation and title level. Managers must not deviate from this written schema.

When a company is smaller (fewer than fifty employees or so) and growing fast, there is often so much fluidity that it can be difficult to implement GLP. Most companies end up doing GLP at 150 or more employees, but that is often too late for effectiveness. The compromise is somewhere in the middle. I recommend starting to think about GLP at twenty-five to fifty employees, and then implementing as soon as is practical after that.

LORD OF THE FLIES

Inevitably conflict arises in any organization. When it does, it is up to you to teach your team members how to give and receive nonviolent feedback, and ensure that they do.

Many managers do not enjoy dealing with people in conflict and therefore instead say, "You two, work it out among yourselves." But unless your team is already proficient at nonviolent communication and radical candor, then the two will likely not be able to work it out on their own. If you continue to stay at arm's length, the result will be…*Lord of the Flies*. The absence of governance leads to civil war. This is not healthy.

To stop this behavior, you must step in to adjudicate when your team members are unable to work it out on their own. Give them one chance to do so. If they are not able to, then step in to decide the issue or mediate the conflict. If you don't want to do it yourself, hire a coach to teach and facilitate the feedback sessions. Whatever you do, do not simply leave the participants on their own to work it out. If you do, you will be responsible for the emotional bloodshed that ensues.

In conclusion, your culture is the behavioral norms of your company. If you are unintentional about how you and others behave, you likely won't enjoy the results. Instead, be intentional. Identify the behaviors that you would like to see. Then document them, model them, hire for them, and enforce them.

PART IV

INFRASTRUCTURE

Just as an efficient city requires comprehensive and trustworthy systems to move its traffic, goods, and by-products, your company requires reliable systems to maintain its data and communications flow. Without a solid infrastructure, your brilliant and talented team members won't be able to function to their full potential. The key components to a solid company infrastructure are a company folder system and wiki, goal-tracking tools, areas of responsibility, no single point of failure, and key performance indicators. Let's break each of those down.

CHAPTER 19: COMPANY FOLDER SYSTEM AND WIKI

It may seem obvious, but every company should have a structured folder system for storing documents, such as Google Drive. Each department should have its own folder, and all team members should have access (at least for viewing, if not editing) to all folders except for the one containing compensation, performance reviews, and performance improvement plans.

You should also create a wiki page, which need be nothing more complicated than a document containing links to all the other important company documents. Make sure that reading the relevant parts of this wiki is part of every employee onboarding. As of this writing, Notion.so is my favorite template for a wiki.

WHEN YOU DO IT TWICE, WRITE IT DOWN

After creating a wiki, the question then becomes, "What should we document?" And here is the painful answer: "Everything."

A well-run company documents every aspect of its operations so that its team members can quickly step into a new role when needed.

Here's an easy way to do this: Whenever you find yourself doing something twice, write down exactly what it is that you did. If you've done something twice, you're likely to need to do it again, and someone else may need to do it too. When it's documented, there are clear instructions to follow, which allow for consistency across employees and client situations. Place these written processes in the company wiki.

Require that all members of the team also follow this practice to share their knowledge.

1. Create a spreadsheet to track all processes.
2. Ask each department head to:
   a. List the processes in their department.
   b. Assign a writer and due date to each process.
      i. Space the due dates out so that each writer need only document one process per week.

3. Each writer links their process write-up to the spreadsheet so that you can verify that all have been created.

If you use this process and spread the writings among the whole company, you can likely document every process in your company within three months.

These written processes then become your company's onboarding curriculum. Each new hire reads all the processes they will be asked to do. You can now safely scale your team, knowing that they will have effective onboarding.

This applies to manager onboarding too. Ryan Breslow, founder and CEO of Bolt, shares: "We have noticed that whenever we hire a new manager, they want to instantly bring in their own processes. But then we lose all of our hard-won institutional knowledge that led to the creation of our original process. So we now require that all managers use the existing Bolt processes for at least three months before making any changes. After they know our system in this way, they are free to make the changes they want to. And yet most make relatively minor changes after that."

CHAPTER 20: GOAL-TRACKING SYSTEM

In each company, dozens of new challenges arise each week. Some might be critical, but others will be mere distractions, cluttering up your team's time and energy. Commit to a systematic goal-tracking system to maintain focus and to prevent the clutter from overwhelming your operation.

INDIVIDUAL

Keep it simple. Evernote, OmniFocus, and Culture Code's Things are great tools to track individual goals and tasks. For maximum benefit, use them to implement the GTD system (chapter 3). They are inexpensive and easy to use.

GROUP

For small groups, there is no need for a dedicated group system—it's easy enough to track company goals in a Google Doc. But as soon as you grow to more than a handful of people, you will need a dedicated group goal-tracking system.

There are many excellent systems. They broadly break down between task tracking (Asana and Trello) and goal tracking (Betterworks, 15Five, and Lattice).

Task-tracking systems are excellent at transforming issues to next actions and tracking progress from meeting to meeting. They're a key part of forming impeccable agreements (chapter 13) between people. Whenever two people form an agreement, it should be recorded in the task-tracking system and have an owner, a comprehensive description, and a due date.

Goal-tracking systems are much better at showing the team their progress over many weeks and months, therefore boosting morale.

Whatever system you choose, be careful to use it judiciously, as it is very common for people to become overwhelmed with actions from your tracking system. When this happens, they'll stop using the system altogether. To avoid this, follow two simple rules:

- Never assign someone an action without them agreeing to it verbally or in writing.
- Encourage people to use a separate (and simpler) tool for tracking their individual actions that aren't being tracked by the group. Group-tracking tools simply have more overhead per action than individualized tools and therefore should only be used sparingly.

Goal-tracking tools are a key part of ensuring an efficient infrastructure, so take the time to find the right system for your company and onboard everyone so it's used effectively.

CHAPTER 21: AREAS OF RESPONSIBILITY (AORS)

"Tragedy of the commons." When several people share responsibility for an action or process, often that action doesn't get done well or at all.

To prevent this from happening, group tasks into functions and assign each function to one—and only one—person. These are your areas of responsibility. Apple pioneered AORs in Silicon Valley, but now most successful tech companies use this method.

Create a document that lists all of the company's functions and, for each, the directly responsible individual. This is the AOR list. It serves as a routing layer for any questions and ensures that no functions fall through the cracks. Make sure everybody in the company knows how to access the list, and update it as new functions arise or as responsibilities shift.

Here's a sample AOR list:

Department	AOR	DRI	Backup
Executive	Schedule and set agenda for weekly business development and team meetings	John	Marlo
	Approve large spends over $1,000	John	Marlo
	With conversation from People Ops, give final approval on hires, compensation, and offers	John	Marlo
	Assess company resources and accurately model growth and capital allocation in financial plan	John	Marlo
	Attend fundraising and VC meetings	John	Marlo
	Finalize company's 3-month goals	John	Marlo
	Make monthly investor call	John	Marlo
	Send investor update emails	John	Marlo
	Maintain AORs	John	Marlo
Development	Assign tasks to the team from the features on the product roadmap	Alan	Matthew
	Set and hit development deadlines	Alan	Matthew
	Manage front-end development	Susie	Alan

Department	AOR	DRI	Backup
	Manage back-end development	Matthew	Alan
	Manage databases	Matthew	Alan
	Manage servers	Matthew	Alan
	Set up and oversee bug-reporting process (for development team, all teams, and customers)	Alan	Matthew
	Create API documentation	Matthew	Susie
	Create and maintain automated API tests	Matthew	Susie
	Carry out development recruiting	Alan	Matthew
	Train all new team members with department-specific onboarding	Alan	Matthew
	With help from People Ops, conduct all offboarding meetings for department members	Alan	Matthew
Product	Develop product roadmap	Jennifer	Susie
	Build feature list from customer and team feedback	Jennifer	Susie
	Create wireframes/comps for product roadmap	Susie	Zack
	Review and approve comps	Jennifer	Susie
	Set product pricing	Jennifer	Susie
	Schedule and run biweekly product-development feedback meeting	Jennifer	Susie
	Create product how-to guides and product documentation	Zack	Susie
	Train all new team members with department-specific onboarding	Jennifer	Susie
	With help from People Ops, conduct all offboarding meetings for department members	Jennifer	Susie
Sales	Ensure that all salespeople are entering all information into CRM	Mark	Aaron
	Present sales pipeline update at team meeting	Mark	Aaron

Department	AOR	DRI	Backup
	Manage external consultants (Jen, Ryan Faber, and Alicia)	Mark	Aaron
	Sell managed services to customers, from proposal to close	Aaron	John
	Field and vet inbound leads	Aaron	John
	Make SaaS sales	John	Michael
	Generate outbound leads (sales development reps)	Michael	Aaron
	Ensure sales quotas	John	Michael
	Develop sales collateral, case studies, FAQs, and other assets to accelerate the sales process	Mark	Aaron
	Document the NeoReach sales process	Mark	Aaron
	Train all new team members with department-specific onboarding	Mark	Aaron
	With help from People Ops, conduct all offboarding meetings for department members	Mark	Aaron
Marketing	Present marketing update at team meeting	Mark	Aaron
	Track marketing KPIs	Mark	Aaron
	Create and maintain content marketing calendar	Mark	Aaron
	Create and maintain weekly newsletter	Mark	Aaron
	Maintain competitive landscape analysis	Mark	Aaron
	Write and post press releases	Mark	Aaron
	Develop and maintain journalist network for press releases	Mark	Aaron
	Develop and maintain web presence (includes website, LinkedIn, AngelList, etc.)	Mark	Aaron
	Train all new team members with department-specific onboarding	Mark	Aaron
	With help from People Ops, conduct all offboarding meetings for department members	Mark	Aaron

Department	AOR	DRI	Backup
Finance/ Legal/Admin	Develop and maintain monthly financials	Marlo	John
	Develop and maintain financial forecast	Marlo	John
	Manage expenses with Expensify	Marlo	John
	Train all new team members with department-specific onboarding	Marlo	John
	Manage bill payments with Bill.com	Marlo	John
	Track and claim accounts receivable	Marlo	John
	Manage payroll with Gusto	Marlo	John
	Develop and maintain insertion order and influencer statements of work	Marlo	John
	Develop, sign, and maintain legal documents including incorporation documents, insurance documents, tax forms, etc.	Marlo	John
	With help from People Ops, conduct all offboarding meetings for department members	Marlo	John
	Handle office insurance, utilities, and related documents	Marlo	John
	Keep reports of employee computers and department budgets	Marlo	John
	Ensure HR compliance: Zenefits, internal HR spreadsheet, handbook	Marlo	John
	Manage company events	Marlo	John
	Keep track of team@company.com	Marlo	John

Notice how each department's tasks are grouped together, the task is succinctly described, and there are both a main person responsible for the task and a backup person. This infrastructure ensures no task falls through the cracks because people thought it was another person's responsibility.

CHAPTER 22: **NO SINGLE POINT OF FAILURE**

A single point of failure is a function that one person performs when no one else has full knowledge of how that function works. If that person becomes sick or leaves the company, functionality suffers. A well-run company has no single point of failure. To create a team with no single points of failure, do two things:

1. Write down all processes. As soon as you or your team members find yourselves doing something for the second time (see chapters 7 and 19), you should write down the steps of that process exactly. Place these written processes in a company-wide wiki.
2. Cross-train a second person for each role. Map each function in the company (from the AORs) to a backup person. Have the backup person co-work with the primary until the backup knows how to perform the role. (Of course, having all the processes already written down will vastly improve this training process. So have your team write down all the processes first.)

It's a good standard practice for at least two people to know how to do any given task in the company so that if the lead person is too busy, is sick, or leaves the company, they can request that the secondary person assume the responsibility. This way, no task should fall through the cracks.

CHAPTER 23: KEY PERFORMANCE INDICATORS (KPIS)

It is critical to objectively measure the performance of the company. You can only manage what you can measure. Key performance indicators (KPIs) allow you to do this. KPIs are the one or two significant metrics for each major function that show the entire team in an instant how the company is doing and where the issues are. Here are some examples:

Department	Metric
Finance	Monthly cash burn; cash in the bank
Sales	Monthly recurring revenue
Engineering	Percentage of tickets closed
Recruiting	Percentage of offers accepted

Determine the company's five or six most significant KPIs, then track them religiously and make them available for the entire company to easily see on a daily basis. Post the metrics on a TV screen in a central place in the office, using a tool such as Geckoboard.

As we learned from Andy Grove, former Intel CEO and author of the book *High Output Management*, it is also important to define and track countermetrics to provide necessary context, because metrics are sometimes optimized to a fault.

For example, engineering tickets will vary in importance, so if your engineers have closed the critical tickets, they're doing better than if they close most tickets but only the easiest ones. Similarly, if half of candidates who accept your job offers are less skilled than the half who decline, then you're doing worse than the raw percentage indicates.

Create and measure your metrics carefully and in context to give your team the best possible view of your company's health.

PART V
COLLABORATION

One of the most dangerous transitions that a company makes is going from fewer than ten team members to more than twenty in a short time. During this time, communication and productivity usually break down. The system of group organization that existed when the company was all sitting in the same room together suddenly no longer works when team members are not all sitting next to one another. Once your company has over twenty team members, you will hire great people, but they won't know what to do, and you will be frustrated by their lack of output.

Luckily there is an answer. It has a time cost. But once you implement it, it will allow your company to become productive again, and it will continue to be effective as your company scales from ten team members to hundreds, thousands, and tens of thousands.

Every successful large technology company uses this system. It has no single name—Google, for example, calls theirs Objectives and Key Results, or OKRs—but the systems are essentially the same from company to company. They share the following key functions:

- Setting vision and goals for the company, each department, and each individual on a regular basis (usually quarterly)
- Communicating that vision and those goals to every team member
- Tracking and reporting progress toward those goals on a regular timetable (usually weekly)

- Eliciting feedback from all team members on what is going right and (much more important) what is not going right and needs to be changed

The system streamlines and organizes

- information flowing out, so the CEO can inform team members of the company's priorities, and
- information flowing in, so team members can provide feedback to the CEO about what is and isn't working.

This information exchange takes place through a deliberate series of goal-oriented meetings, which compose the core of the system.

In my experience, it is very easy to copy this system if you see it in operation. But it is very difficult to implement such a system by reading instructions (including these). When you get to this point in your company's life cycle, I recommend doing one of two things:

- Hire a COO who was a manager at a large, well-managed company (over two hundred employees) to implement and run this system for you
- Hire an ex-CEO to come in as a one-day-a-week CEO to implement this system. This person should be able to do so in eight to twelve weeks. Have this person then watch you run the system for two weeks to ensure that you are doing it correctly. Then run it yourself going forward.

The chapters in this part give you a blueprint for such a system. But, again, it is impossible for me to convey in writing the detail and nuance. The following chapters serve more as a notional checklist than a set of instructions.

One of the measures of your having successfully implemented this system is that your original team members continue to perform as excellent managers even as their departments grow massively. If there is no system, then you will be forced to hire ever-more-experienced managers who will layer over your original team members. When that happens, a tremendous amount of institutional knowledge is lost, and ultimately the company can never perform as well.

This dichotomy is clear when looking at NBA teams. The Golden State Warriors were a mediocre team under coach Mark Jackson. Once Steve Kerr joined as coach in 2014 and brought an effective system, the exact same roster of players became dominant and won the championship. (Yes, they brought in Kevin Durant, but that was only later.) By contrast, the Cleveland Cavaliers and Houston Rockets had no system and simply relied on individual talent. Even against remarkable talent, the system inevitably wins.

The dichotomy can be seen in companies as well. Many members of Facebook's original leadership team continue to be on the leadership team today. This is because Sheryl Sandberg brought a management system to the company that elevated all who used it. By contrast, Twitter has not developed a similarly effective system. Instead they have hired individual superstars. And while the people at Twitter are remarkably talented, the company as a whole does not function nearly as well as Facebook.

CHAPTER 24: **ORGANIZATIONAL STRUCTURE**

In the early stage of a company, before product-market fit, when your team is six people or fewer, there is little value in creating a formal organizational structure or in creating a distinction among co-founders as to who the CEO is. But when product-market fit is achieved, it is time to scale rapidly.

Once you have achieved product-market fit, that is the right time to blitzscale and win the race to market share. You're going to need to diversify your skills and grow your team. To do this, you will need to create massive awareness (marketing), walk many customers through the sales process (sales), hold those customers' hands as they set up and use your product or service (customer success), harden your infrastructure to withstand many users at once (DevOps), get rid of technical debt and add all the features promised in your roadmap (engineering), update the product roadmap to meet the most urgent needs of your customers (product), and all the nontechnical operations (people [recruiting, training, and HR], finance, legal, office). All of this requires hiring talented and experienced people to fulfill those functions. First raise the money needed to hire this team, and then begin hiring.

Once you bring on remote workers and your team scales beyond fifteen to twenty people, it's common for things to begin to fall apart. You could hire very talented people, and they simply won't perform in the way that you hope or expect. You could end up doing more and more work yourself, working longer and longer hours, just to keep the company afloat. You might extrapolate this trend and realize that soon you will break.

That is the reason you need to implement a formal management system. It will be painful. You will no longer be able to just "work on the product." You and your team will likely have to spend one full day per week preparing for and participating in team and one-on-one meetings. These meetings and this system will feel like pure overhead. They are. And without them, your company will never scale successfully.

The good news is that the same system that allows your company to operate well with twenty-five people will also allow it to work well with twenty-five thousand. Neither the system nor the amount of overhead will change. It is a one-time hit.

To create this formal management system, start by delineating separate teams, each with a manager. The organizational structure should be determined by who attends what team meeting.

The leadership team typically consists of the following people:

1. CEO
2. Head of product
3. Head of engineering
4. Head of sales
5. Head of marketing
6. Head of customer success
7. Head of operations (people [recruiting, training, and HR], finance, legal, and office)

Each of these department heads then has a team that they manage. Once you adopt an organizational structure, write it down and make it public to the company. There should be no confusion about who reports to whom and what team meeting each person attends.

CEO

If you find that you are simply not completing the goals you set for yourself each week, or that you do so but some or many of the tasks are energy-draining, then it is time to hire a COS.

In a *First Round Review* article titled "Why You Need Two Chiefs in the Executive Office," Mark Organ, CEO of Influitive, gives a thorough description of COS best practices. To me, the two priorities in creating a great COS are (1) their background and (2) how you train them.

When it comes to background, the best chiefs of staff that I have seen are highly organized, are excellent communicators (both written and oral), and have broad strategic business knowledge. A background that almost always ensures these skills is four to eight years at a top management consulting firm (e.g., Bain, BCG, or McKinsey). I am partial to Bain, as I find ex-Bain consultants also have excellent financial modeling skills (akin to those they would have learned had they worked as an associate at an investment bank).

On training, the key is to give your COS unfettered access to all the information that you receive. This means having your COS sit beside you from morning till night, with full access to your emails, calls, meetings, and so on. By seeing what decisions you make, based on what information you receive, your COS will soon be able to think like you and can truly be an extension of you (and magic will happen).

After several weeks of observing, your COS can start to take tasks off your plate. Within several months, your COS will be able to do all the tasks that don't give you energy, or that you simply don't have the band-width to do.

Most senior candidates are not attracted to the COS role because they view it as an assistant role (and in many companies it is). When you're recruiting, dispel this concern by showing the candidate that they will have full access to all the information that you do. Being a COS in this capacity is the single best training for becoming a CEO (or head of any department) that exists.

BIZ OPS

As your company quickly scales, the young people you hired early in the company's life cycle will be asked to manage bigger and bigger teams. Some will learn to be good managers fast enough. Others won't.

In dealing with those who don't, you will be in a difficult situation. You want to be transparent with them that they are not succeeding. And then when you decide to layer them, you will also want to be transparent with them so that they can be your partner in the search. (They will find out anyway once you start recruiting and will feel betrayed if you didn't already inform them.) You will likely feel fear that they will become de-motivated and perform even worse (or leave) before you are able to hire, train, and onboard their replacement. (This fear is usually overblown, as most young managers look forward to learning from someone more expe-rienced.) But whether or not you feel this fear, the reality is that you want the team's performance to improve now, and recruiting a new manager from the outside will take time. Much more time than you would like. So how do you improve the team's performance now?

There is an answer.

In Silicon Valley, major tech companies such as Google and LinkedIn built up functions called business operations. The functions were staffed mainly by top-tier consultants from Bain, McKinsey, and BCG. I first encountered BizOps at Coinbase, where Emilie Choi scaled the group out as the company was going through hypergrowth. The team was viewed as mini-CEOs who could provide the following support:

- Parachute into any problem area, dig in, and fix it
- Generally help build and drive processes that help the company scale, including running quarterly business reviews, setting OKRs and KPIs
- When a manager is not succeeding, join that manager's team and take over the project and people management duties while keeping the former manager as the architect (i.e., the subject matter expert who determines the roadmap: "These are the things that we need to get done, and this is how to do them") and managing the team to ensure the roadmap is completed
- Effectively run any meeting and train managers how to do so
- Act as chief of staff to the CEO

Creating these functions has been a big success for Coinbase. I highly recommend that you designate a team to carry out these functions.

BOARD OF DIRECTORS

The board of directors is related to the executive department. By law, C corporations must a have a board of directors, which must meet regularly in order to be informed about the company's operations and provide fiduciary oversight. Organizations are incorporated in order to shield their owners from personal liability for the debts of the company.

It is important to have a partner or set of thought partners to keep you accountable when it comes to picking the best goals and then marching toward those goals. This can be a coach, an advisory board, or your actual board. As a corporation, you must have regular board meetings. Therefore, if you trust and like your actual board members, then making them your thought partners is best practice. If that is the case, then I recommend that you follow the best-practice model below. If you do not have full trust in your board, I highly recommend that you get to a place of full trust through facilitation or replacing board members. But if you are still unable to create the board of full trust right now, then follow the minimal model below.

BEST PRACTICE

The best board meeting is one that gives board members enough information to allow them to be useful to you. Be transparent. Be vulnerable. If you do, you will be rewarded with rich and useful feedback.

Here are my board meeting best practices:

1. Share the board meeting information (the board packet) with all board members in writing in advance of the meeting.
    a. Format: Memo or deck (My preference is memo, as it lends itself more to reading.)
    b. Days in advance: Delivered to the board at least three days in advance, but ideally one week in advance
    c. Information included:
        i. Update on KPIs:
            a.) Summary financials
            b.) Product roadmap
            c.) Hiring roadmap
            d.) Sales pipeline
        ii. What we accomplished last quarter (OKRs)
        iii. From both KPIs and OKRs:
            a.) What went (or is going) well
            b.) What didn't go (or isn't going) well
                i.) Why
                ii.) What we are doing to fix it
        iv. What we hope to accomplish this quarter (OKRs)
        v. Issues: One or two strategic questions or problems that we are grappling with (could be from the update above)
            a.) The issue or choice written out thoroughly
            b.) Our proposed solution

        i.) Most board members have useful pattern-matching advice on forward-looking strategic questions (e.g., should we expand to Europe? Should we launch an adjacent product?) but don't have enough detailed knowledge of the particular situation to opine on internal operating issues (e.g., our CMO is struggling, what should we do?). Stick to the forward-looking questions in the board meeting.

    vi. Requests

      a.) Specific action requests of board members

        i.) Most board members have strong networks. Take advantage of this by asking for warm introductions to potential customers, partners, recruits, and other investors.

    vii. Feedback

      a.) How could the company's and CEO's interaction with the board be better?

2. Collect responses.

    a. Ask board members to pose questions about and write responses to the board packet at least two days before the meeting.

    b. During the next forty-eight hours, you or your internal team write answers to all board member questions.

3. Meet (phone call) with board members one-on-one just before the board meeting.

    a. Ensure that they have digested the information.

    b. Elicit their questions and concerns so that they come to the board meeting already feeling heard (this is critical for creating trust).

4. At the board meeting:

    a. Invite the executive team to attend. This allows board members and executives to get to know one another and gain comfort with one another.

    b. Spend the first fifteen minutes allowing board members to read the responses to all board packet questions.

    c. Unpack one strategic question or issue.

      i. Ask for each board member's view. Give equal airtime.

      ii. Board observers and lawyers do not speak unless you specifically ask for their input.

    d. Unpack the second issue.

e. Confirm that each board member is willing to do the actions requested.

f. Collect written feedback, if it wasn't already collected in the response to the board packet.

5. Have social time.

a. It is often healthy to create an informal social venue for board members and the executive team to interact. This is usually a meal before or after the meeting.

b. Board observers and lawyers are usually not invited to this gathering.

MINIMAL

Use this method if you are still working on creating a board you fully trust:

1. Keep the board to an odd number of seats (to avoid a deadlocked vote) and as few seats as possible. The ideal number is three. Try very hard not to go beyond five.

2. Board observers are supposed to observe only during a board meeting and not talk unless asked a direct question by a board member. Enforce this behavior.

3. Give the board members all the information they need at a board meeting (or even better, before the board meeting) in writing so that they have few or no questions during the meeting. Here is the best way to do this:

a. Create a very complete presentation with the following information:

i. Full financials and metrics/KPIs

ii. The good and the bad from these metrics

iii. What we accomplished since the last board meeting (OKRs)

iv. What we plan to accomplish until the next board meeting (OKRs)

v. Major challenges that we face and how we plan to address them

b. Do a test run with a trusted non–board member who asks questions about anything that is unclear. Answer all their questions, and add the answers to the board presentation.

c. Present this final version to the board, and they will likely have no further questions.

4. After the board presentation, where there are hopefully few to no questions, give the board members homework. Give each one a very specific assignment. Don't worry, none of them will actually do the homework. They also are then not likely to give you unsolicited advice. This is the true goal of the homework.

5. If a board member does give you advice, take notes. Summarize what the board member said, and ask if you got it right. Once they say, "Yes, that's right," thank them for their advice and let them know that you will seriously consider it in formulating your plan for going forward. This will make the board member feel that you at least heard them, which is primarily what they are after.

PRODUCT DEPARTMENT

In a technology company, the product manager is arguably the most important position in the company. For this reason, in the past decade, most unicorns have been started by technical founders where at least one has the ability to play the role of product manager.

A product manager is someone who both has the social skills to sit with customers and is (or can learn to be) technical enough to know what can and cannot be done technically. Whether the product manager has to have a background as an engineer is a hot point of contention. Some say that there is no other way; others say that it doesn't really matter. From my experience, technical knowledge is very helpful; however, it is not a deal breaker, especially if the product manager has a good relationship with the technical lead and together they can solve problems honestly and efficiently.

The product manager has several roles:

1. Sit with real-life potential and actual customers and deeply get to know the customer's life and problems. Because the product manager is technical, they know what features are possible (and how hard or easy they are to create) and can then list a set of features that will solve a customer's deepest problems. The product manager then assigns an initial order to the features in the list according to the value they bring to the customer and the difficulty for the engineering team to create them.

2. Lead the product meeting that brings together engineering (those who

have to build it) and sales and marketing (those who have to sell it) to determine the final order of the feature list to be built. High-value, low-cost features clearly come first. High-cost, low-value features clearly come last. The debate is in the middle. And here the right answer is most often high-value, high-cost before low-value, low-cost.

3. Map out wireframes (which are illustrations of what the feature will physically look like when completed) and specifications (of how the feature functions) for each feature so that the engineering team has a visual and functional picture of what they need to build. Engineers do best when given a very specific end point. Allow them the room to figure out how to get to that end point, but be very clear about what the end point is.

Number 3 requires a lot of time spent with engineering to get their feedback as to whether the wireframes and specs are complete enough to give the direction needed. Engineering is the customer in this exercise. For this reason, there is often a tendency to think that product should report to engineering. This would be a mistake.

Product must have the final authority in the discussion around feature prioritization. If either engineering or sales and marketing has the authority, the decision will get skewed. Ideally, therefore, product is its own department and reports directly to the CEO.

If, for some strange reason, product cannot report directly to the CEO, then better to have it report to sales and marketing. It is critical that the voice of the customer remain strong within the company. This voice almost always gets lost if product reports to engineering.

The best product managers also paint a picture for engineers of why a feature is actually needed by a customer. Engineers are smart. They want to know that what they are building has actual value. To do this, complete the end user profile described in Bill Aulet's *Disciplined Entrepreneurship*. Clearly show (in writing) how this feature will solve a significant problem for the customer.

ENGINEERING DEPARTMENT

For most startups, the biggest challenge in engineering is managing the team once it grows beyond three to four engineers. A good engineer is often not a good engineering manager.

There are three functions within engineering: architect, project manager, and individual contributor. Project management is the essential skill of the engineering manager.

Good engineering management is a rare skill and most often can only be learned by observing others who do it well. Therefore, hire an engineering manager who has experience at a company with a reputation for excellent engineering management (Google, Facebook, Apple, etc.). Engineering managers with this pedigree will be hard to convince and expensive to win. Make the effort and pay the price. It's worth it!

Another common problem is that adding engineers often adds significant coordination challenges. These challenges create a net drag on productivity. Unless you have a superior manager, a team of three to four excellent engineers is often more productive than that same team with an additional three to four average engineers.

In order to manage an engineering team effectively, a good tracking tool must be used (just as in sales tracking). The industry standard is JIRA by Atlassian. Once you get to ten to twenty-five engineers, this tool is a must, but it requires knowledge and time to use properly. When the team is smaller, I recommend using a lighter-weight tool.

SALES, MARKETING, AND CUSTOMER SUCCESS DEPARTMENTS

While these are all technically their own departments with their own leads, they're all related to interfacing with customers to support sustainable relationships with them. These departments have unique approaches and tactics, so be sure your team leads have applicable skill sets. For tips on running sales and marketing departments successfully, see chapter 30.

OPERATIONS DEPARTMENT

The operations department reports to the CEO and has four subdepartments: people (recruiting, training, and HR), finance, legal, and office. Let's take a closer look at some of these subdepartments.

HUMAN RESOURCES

On the HR side, there are specific laws that must be adhered to when hiring and firing. You can take the time to learn these laws (not recommended), or you can simply outsource the process. There are two ways to outsource the HR process:

1. Use an online broker like Rippling to manage the documentation and purchase benefits (medical, dental, disability, and life insurance).
2. Use a professional employer organization (PEO) like Sequoia One or TriNet. If you use a PEO, members of your team become employees of the PEO.

I recommend using a PEO from the beginning until the company reaches 100–150 people in size.

A PEO has thousands of "employees" and therefore can get far better pricing on benefits (insurance) than a small company with fewer than one hundred employees. Additionally a PEO takes on all the employee liability risk. If employees are let go and sue their employer, they sue the PEO. Your company is not involved at all. The PEO ensures that they will not lose such a lawsuit by adhering 100 percent to HR law. The PEO is expert in this compliance.

Once a company has reached 100–150 employees, it can achieve similar prices for benefits, and it can afford to hire an HR specialist. Then it is time to switch back to the company being the employer and providing the benefits directly (using Rippling or something similar as the information platform). This allows team members to direct their questions to an HR specialist who is on-site rather than off-site.

What benefits to offer? This depends on the types of team members being recruited.

From the team members' perspective, benefits are paid with pretax dollars, effectively doubling their purchase power. Discover what your team members truly value (medical insurance, meals, retirement plan, gym membership, commuting allowance, etc.) and then give them those benefits. Of course, the cost of the benefit should be taken out of the overall compensation number. Thus, startup cash plus equity plus benefits should equal market compensation (which also should include benefits).

If PEOs are so great, why aren't they used more often in startups? Good question. I think that most founders just don't know about them. Also, simple online tools like Gusto and Rippling make the process of hiring and paying employees so easy that most founders stop there. The thought of lowering HR liability and reducing benefit costs comes later. And by that time, the CEO is focused on other more pressing issues, like product. It usually takes a full-time CFO to make the change to a PEO, but the CFO often only arrives once the company has more than fifty employees, and then the benefit of a PEO is not nearly as great.

Instead, I recommend starting with a PEO when the benefit is highest: at the beginning.

FINANCE

A company needs to track its revenue and expenses (income statement), as well as its assets and liabilities (balance sheet). This task is easy enough in the early days that a full-time person is not needed. So it is best to outsource this function. SaaS accounting tools (e.g., QuickBooks Online) make this process seamless. Many accounting shops will do this work off-site for a reasonable fee (less than $2,000 per month). However, the work product improves significantly if the work is done on-site because of better communication and oversight. So choose an outsourced CFO or accounting firm that is willing to send a person to your office (once per month or week) to do the accounting work.

In addition, a company should be creating a projection of both its finances and its operations (number and type of employees, amount of office space), as well as tracking the metrics of the team. This is considered CFO-level work. Any good CFO can also do the accounting work. I recommend hiring an outsourced CFO firm rather than an outsourced accounting firm.

Potential investors take great comfort in seeing that a company has created real projections, which is a signal that the company won't be blindsided by unforeseen occurrences in the future.

LEGAL

There are several actions within a company that require the help of a lawyer: negotiating and documenting investments (whether a simple agreement for future equity or preferred equity), establishing hiring and firing procedures (to comply with HR law), negotiating and signing customer contracts (nondisclosure agreements and commercial contracts), obtaining visas for foreign team members, and so on.

There are many large multidiscipline law firms that are very familiar to investors (Wilson Sonsini, Cooley, Orrick, Fenwick & West, Goodwin Procter, etc.) and with whom investors feel comfortable. Therefore, it is a good idea to use such a law firm to document any preferred equity investment. The additional cost for this law firm is more than paid for by the benefit in making your investors feel comfortable.

However, that is where the utility of using the big law firm ends. While the big law firm has the resources to do every kind of legal work the company has, the amount that they will charge for this work is (in my experience) about ten times what could be achieved by working with specialist boutiques and solo practitioners. And the specialists usually do better work.

So the key is to find a solo practitioner to be your outsourced general counsel early on in the company's life cycle. I prefer to find a lawyer who lives and works close to the company and then require that they come into the office to do their work (and only bill for their time physically at the company). If there is a need to do legal work remotely, I recommend that you pay for it only if the lawyer has gotten specific written permission (email) in advance for both the work and the hours to be billed.

If you don't follow this strict procedure, then the lawyer can bill for whatever amount of hours they claim the work took. You will have no way of successfully disputing their claim. And you will be on the hook for the bill, even if it is outrageous (which it almost certainly will be).

Solo practitioners are happy to follow these guidelines. Large law firms never agree to them. And because lawyers from large law firms do not come on-site, the amount of time they spend on an issue (or at least claim they spend on an issue) goes up by five times over someone who is on-site. Add on top of that the fact that large law firm billing rates are about two times those for solo practitioners, and you get a bill that is ten times larger and a work product that is often inferior.

Once you have an outsourced general counsel who comes to your office to do all of your legal work, if a different specialty is needed (immigration, employment, etc.), they can find and manage that specialist for you.

OTHER ORGANIZATIONAL DETAILS

Now that you have the overall structure, you'll also need to think about how you'll handle related details like job titles, leadership versus VP meetings, and reorganizations. Some of these will be relevant right away (like titles), and some will be implemented as you scale even more.

TITLES

BY ALEX MACCAW

When you're first starting out, it can be quite tempting to hand out titles without much process; after all, they're free. However, a misplaced title can come back to haunt you. Take, for example, the circumstance of making a senior hire and asking an existing team member to report to them. If you've already handed that existing team member a fancy title, this will be viewed as a demotion and you may lose them.

One easy solution is to call everyone "head of X." That way, when it's finally time to hire senior VPs, they can slot easily into the organization without "demoting" anyone.

REORGANIZATIONS

Reorgs, like terminations, are always disruptive and cause people angst, even if the logic for them is glaringly obvious. Full buy-in is impossible to achieve because you cannot solicit opinions from a wide group of people beforehand. Department heads should indeed be consulted ahead of time and then asked to prepare for the rollout, but this consulting or prep time should be very short (to minimize leakage of the reorg prior to the announcement). The exercise then becomes akin to group crisis therapy. The key is that the detailed explanation and Q&A session (first in the all-hands meeting, and then moving to departments and finally individual teams in both a group meeting and then one-on-ones for each team member) should happen immediately after the announcement of the reorg.

A second key is to batch organizational changes. The organization will need time to heal. Even if you recognize needed organizational changes six weeks later, batch them. I recommend three months as a bare minimum between organizational changes, but six months is better.

The organizational structure, while important, isn't as important as the culture and systems you build within it. The best corporations emphasize accountability, coaching, and transparency, and they use a meeting system built on these principles and organized for efficiency. The next chapters will go into these concepts in detail.

CHAPTER 25: ACCOUNTABILITY, COACHING, AND TRANSPARENCY

Now that you have your organizational structure set, everybody understands how it works, and various related details like job titles and the leadership team are clarified, it's time to put your focus on a structured meeting system.

For an organization to work well, three things must occur at every level of the organization and be apparent at every meeting:

- Accountability
- Coaching
- Transparency

These form an easy-to-remember acronym: ACT.

Accountability is declaring

- a destination (vision, OKRs, KPIs);
- the action steps to get there (actions); and
- whether those actions steps were taken (and eventually the destination achieved).

Coaching is declaring

- the current health of the entity (individual, team, department, company), both the good and the not good; and
- with the not good, what the issue is in detail and a proposed solution. (This is where reports can make requests for help from their manager.)

Transparency is declaring (to a person's manager, peers, and reports) feedback to people on what they are doing, using the following framework:

- Like: "These are the specific actions that I like that you are doing."
- Wish that: "These are the specific actions that I wish you would do differently."

This accountability, coaching, and transparency needs to happen in both directions (from CEO to the company, and from the company to the CEO) and at every level (company, department, team, and individual). This is best achieved through a series of weekly meetings. We'll cover them in more detail in the next chapter, but I want to emphasize here that each manager should plan to devote a full day each week to internal meetings. The overhead—20 percent of the standard workweek—can feel tremendous to a startup CEO who is accustomed to the organic information flow of a small group working together in the same room. But without this one-day-per-week investment, a larger team will never fully know what to do, nor will the CEO get the needed feedback on their performance or the company's performance.

CALENDAR CADENCE

If we're planning to spend one day a week in internal meetings, we'll also have to spend some time in external meetings—typically with new-hire candidates—and those won't fit in the same day and will spill over into other parts of the week. With that in mind, it's important to be realistic about the toll that having meetings on multiple days per week can have on departments, particularly engineering.

Paul Graham of Y Combinator points out that makers (engineers) need long stretches of uninterrupted time to be productive, whereas managers are most effective when meeting. The compromise is to schedule days when no meetings are allowed. The schedule that works best for a five-day workweek is as follows:

- One day of internal meetings
- One day of external meetings (e.g., interviewing candidates)
- Three days of no meetings

It isn't critical when these days are, although it helps to space the two meeting days apart from each other.

The above schedule often comes under fire from recruiters who worry that conducting all on-site interviews on a single day will be difficult and many qualified candidates won't be able to make it in on the appointed day. This shouldn't be a real concern, for a couple of reasons.

First, your hire and close rate for candidates who are interviewed in person should be very high (approximately 75 percent); otherwise, you are losing incredible amounts of time by doing all-day in-person interviews with many candidates whom you don't want to hire or who don't want to work for you. Therefore, unless you are already hitting the 75 percent metric, you should start screening candidates more effectively (i.e., brutally) in your phone interviews and lower the number of in-person interviews.

Second, it is true that some candidates can only come in on specific days. However, the benefits of having meetings on only one set day, as measured by increased productivity of the company, far outweigh the cost of losing out on a few candidates. Additionally, if the candidate cannot find the time to make it on the set day within two or three weeks, it is quite likely that they won't take the job anyway. There are many other high-level candidates out there. You can find another one. But there is only a finite number of productive work hours within the company. Once lost, there is no way to recapture them. For more on recommended recruiting and screening practices, please see chapter 29.

There are two exceptions to the advice above:

- In the very early days of a company when a department has just one person, the department lead can set a recruiting schedule that works for them as they build their team.
- Departments that are entirely nontechnical and don't require focused work time can set their own recruiting schedule.

The guidelines above are for when there is already a team in place that requires uninterrupted days for its work. This is particularly important for the engineering team.

CHAPTER 26: **MEETINGS**

When creating the schedule for the day of internal meetings, I recommend the following order:

1. One-on-one meetings
2. Leadership team meeting
3. CEO open office hour
4. All-hands meeting
5. Company-wide social event

Start the meeting day with the weekly one-on-one meetings. The weekly leadership team meeting will be the longest (up to three hours in the beginning, until the team learns the habit of writing down all input before the meeting, and then it can get down to thirty minutes). The CEO open office hour, all-hands meeting, and company-wide social event will consume the remainder of the day. The one-day limit for all internal meetings directly relates to how many team members a single manager can effectively oversee. If one of your managers can't fit all the necessary meetings into a single day, they have too many people reporting directly to them and you need to reorganize, or they need to run more efficient meetings.

As the company grows and each department becomes its own team, have each department do their meeting on a day other than that of the CEO's meeting day. Department meeting days serve as preparation for the CEO's meeting day (updates, issues, etc.) and therefore should occur before the CEO's meeting day.

And as the company begins to have subteams, schedule their meeting day before the department meeting day.

MEETING LEADS

Each meeting needs to have a designated meeting lead, who is sometimes, but not always, the group's manager. This person is responsible for making the meeting run well. Therefore, their tasks are as follows:

- Publishing the agenda, hoped-for outcome, and attendee list of the meeting to all participants
- Ensuring that all meeting participants submit their updates and issues in writing in advance and show up on time
- Ruthlessly sticking to the timeline during the meeting and, whenever something off-topic comes up, noting it but scheduling the discussion for another time

Without an effective meeting lead, meetings quickly become inefficient, and people come to resent them.

WEEKLY MEETINGS

So if the basics for all meetings are to have focused, efficient meeting leads and to achieve accountability, coaching, and transparency, what do the various meetings look like? Here's the breakdown.

ONE-ON-ONE MEETINGS

One-on-one meetings are a time to ensure that each employee is fully prepared for the team meeting. (As reports begin to prepare fully for their one-on-one meeting in advance, then their accountability and coaching can be pushed into the team meeting, allowing more time for transparency during the one-on-one meeting.)

I recommend that all team members read the same book to get on the same page about what the purpose and structure of these meetings will be. If you manage managers, then that book should be the best one: Andy Grove's *High Output Management*. This book is the gold standard for how to effectively manage a team. But it is not short. If you manage individual contributors who are unlikely to read a long book, then instead ask the team to read *The One Minute Manager* by Kenneth Blanchard and Spencer Johnson. It's a very short read (thirty minutes), and it contains simple, effective advice. Assigning it uniformly will make sure your whole team has a common basis for proceeding.

A new hire's first one-on-one meeting should occur soon after the onboarding process is complete. Have both the manager and the team member come to the meeting with written, measurable OKRs (or a ninety-day roadmap) for the new team member. When the manager and team member reach a consensus on a set of OKRs (ideally three or fewer), merge these into one list.

Run subsequent meetings according to the following template.

TEAM MEMBER

1. Accountability (goals and actions)
   a. Last week
      i. For each of your stated actions from last week, did you get them done—yes or no?
         a.) If no, what blocked you?
         b.) What habit can you adopt so that you don't encounter that obstacle again?
   b. Next week
      i. For each of your OKRs, what one action can you take to advance toward each of them?
2. Coaching (issues and solutions)
   a. Show your OKRs in traffic-light fashion (green, yellow, red).
      i. Green = on track
      ii. Yellow = slightly off track
      iii. Red = far off track
   b. Show your KPIs in traffic-light fashion.
   c. Show any pipelines that are relevant (recruiting, sales, customer success, engineering roadmap, etc.).
   d. If I were to dig into these updates, what would I discover in your department that is:
      i. Good?
      ii. Not good?
         a.) Please describe the issue in detail, as well as your proposed solution. This proposed solution should include:
            i.) What you can do to solve the issue
            ii.) What I (your manager) can do to help unblock you
   e. Please list any other issues that you see in the company, with peers, with the product, in your own life, etc.

    i.   For each, please list your proposed solution. Even if you are unsure of what the right course of action is, take a stab at a definitive roadmap. It will help advance the conversation.

3. Transparency (feedback)
   a. What did you like that I did as manager?
   b. What do you wish that I would do differently as manager?
      i.   Please think of the feedback that you are afraid to give me because you think that it will hurt my feelings. Please give me that feedback.

MANAGER

1. Transparency
   a. Get feedback from your report.
      i.   Elicit negative feedback about your actions. Do this any way you can. Ask for it, appreciate it, and act on it. This is the key to making a team member feel heard and valued.
      ii. Once you have gotten critical feedback, then either:
         a.) Accept
            i.) If you accept, cocreate a written action step that you can take to act on it. Put this action step on your group task manager so that your report can see that you actually do it.
         b.) Not accept
            i.) In some rare cases, there will be feedback that you do not accept. That is okay, as long as you are clear about why you do not accept the request.
   b. Give feedback to your report.
      i.   Since the previous meeting, state what actions your report did that you liked. Be specific.
      ii. State what actions you wish that your report would do differently. State these as specific future actions.
         a.) For example, "I wish that you would ask for feedback from your direct reports in your one-on-ones."
   c. Update the team member's goals:

i. Ensure that the OKRs are still relevant.

ii. Ensure that their declared actions for the upcoming week are the straightest line to achieving their OKRs.

iii. Ensure that their proposed solutions are the straightest line to solving the issue.

iv. Ensure that they have copied and pasted all their actions (from OKRs and issues and solutions) into the group task manager.

Schedule these meetings regularly, at a fixed day and time. The schedule is usually weekly but can be biweekly or even monthly once team members develop expertise at their tasks if their goals remain consistent over time. Another alternative is to set different paces for accountability, coaching, and transparency—for example, meet weekly for coaching and transparency, but do accountability on a biweekly or monthly cadence.

On your company's day for internal meetings, schedule one-on-one meetings before the team meeting. Schedule them back-to-back, and allot twenty-five to fifty minutes for each one. If there is a serious issue to discuss, such as job dissatisfaction, then use your open office hour (see below) later that day to fully address the issue.

One-on-one meetings and team meetings can be merged if a team is small enough, but be cautious about giving negative feedback in a group setting. Unless your team has agreed to radical transparency and actively wants this public negative feedback, shame is likely to arise. Most companies, therefore, opt to provide negative feedback only during one-on-one meetings.

That being said, I do recommend moving to a culture of radical transparency. Doing so will allow you to merge all one-on-one meetings into the team meeting. This can save you four to six hours on your day of internal meetings.

But radical transparency first requires explicit buy-in from every team member and training in how to do it effectively. The Conscious Leadership Group runs excellent one-day trainings in radical transparency. The investment of time may seem large but usually pays itself back within a few weeks (e.g., by saving a half day per week of long one-on-ones).

At the leadership team meeting, the CEO and key decision makers discuss issues that came up during the leader one-on-ones or the department one-on-ones. This is the time to address all issues and either resolve them or move them to a RAPID decision-making process. All nonsensitive decisions from the leadership team meeting can then be shared at the all-hands meeting.

In order to support the company's quarterly goals, each team must meet weekly (or biweekly if the team runs very smoothly), following the ACT model:

- Hold each other accountable to the actions they need to perform.
- Surface and resolve any issues in the company.
- Give each other feedback.

During the leadership team meeting, here is what each attendee should do:

1. Report whether they accomplished their declared actions from the previous meeting. This should be a simple yes or no. If no, they should also write why they didn't do the action and what habit they can adopt to make sure they never encounter that obstacle again. Here is an example:
   a. Get feedback from Joe. *No*
      i. *Why? I forgot about it and therefore didn't ask for feedback when I met with Joe.*
      ii. *Habit? Create an Agenda list. Look at this list each time I meet with someone.*
2. Report their department updates.
   a. Show:
      i. Link to traffic-lighted KPIs
      ii. Link to traffic-lighted OKRs
   b. The written update should be a deep dive into these metrics to share what has happened that is:
      i. Good
      ii. Not good
         a.) What exactly is the issue?

b.) What is your proposed solution for correcting the issue?

    i.) Many people will say that they do not know what the solution is and want guidance. That is fine. But the discussion will be much more fruitful if they declare definitively what they think the solution is, even if they have very little confidence in their proposal.

3. Declare what actions they will do until the next meeting.
    a. Actions toward their OKRs
    b. Actions as part of proposed solutions
4. Provide feedback to the team leader and peers in the "like" and "wish that" format.
    a. Peer to peer
        i. Each peer gives feedback to one other peer per meeting (on a rotating basis).
    b. Reports to manager
        i. If these were done in the one-on-one, then it is good to show them in the leadership team meeting.
    c. Manager to reports
        i. Do this only if the company is practicing radical transparency; otherwise, this remains in the one-on-one.

The agenda for the leadership team meeting then looks like this:

1. Updates from each team member (1, 2, and 3 from above)
2. Discussion of issues and proposed solutions
    a. Time-box each issue.
        i. If a solution is agreed on in that time, turn it into action items with DRIs and due dates.
        ii. If a solution is not agreed on, turn the issue into a RAPID.
3. Feedback to each other (write and review)

Leadership team meetings follow the same information flow as the one-on-one meetings: accountability, coaching, and transparency. In fact, as the leadership team is effectively preparing in writing in advance for its meetings, the accountability and coaching portions of the one-on-ones can simply be moved to the team meeting. This is actually more effective and efficient, allowing more time during the one-on-ones for transparency.

When the company grows to the point of needing department meetings each week too, those meetings would follow this same format.

It is important to time-box all agenda items so that the meetings don't run on and so that all issues get addressed. This is done by putting a number before each agenda item. Five minutes is indicated as [5]. At the end of the allotted time, move on. If there are still decisions to be made, create a RAPID.

It is critical that everyone submit all their updates, issues, and feedback in writing before the meeting, as discussed in chapter 12, "Decision-Making." This allows others to read the submissions, make comments, and ask questions before the meeting. This massively increases information flow and allows for consensus to be reached before the leadership team meeting even begins. Leadership team meetings that take three hours when done verbally can take thirty minutes (and be more effective) when done in writing.

Leadership versus VPs Meeting

As the company grows, each team will become a large entity (BizOps, design, communications, compliance, etc.). An individual product may grow large enough to warrant being its own business unit with its own general manager. Thus there will be many VP-level execs. You will want to keep them informed and empowered. You will be tempted to invite them to attend the leadership team meeting. Do not.

If someone needs to attend a meeting in order to be informed about what occurs in that meeting, then you have not yet created a transparent system. Each meeting should have clear notes of all updates given and all decisions made (other than those around an individual's compensation or performance improvement). Those notes should be freely published to the company so that everyone can know what happened in a meeting without actually attending.

The meeting then just becomes a way of making good and fast decisions.

The leadership team meeting should be attended by your brain trust. Who are the key minds you need to hear from to make great decisions?

And who runs the major business units that you need to make sure are continually unblocked? These should be the attendees of the leadership team meeting. Do not add any other attendees to salve their ego. They will just make the meeting less efficient.

For all the rest of your department and team leads, there is a VPs meeting (or leads meeting). At this meeting, decisions that were just made in the leadership team meeting are announced. There is then a "speak now or forever hold your peace" moment. If any of these decisions will have unintended negative consequences, now is the time for the VPs to raise their hand and say, "That is a terrible idea for these reasons..." The decision then gets kicked into a RAPID. But for the vast majority of decisions, the VPs will be fine with it, and then the decision gets published to the company and announced in the all-hands meeting.

To understand the scale of these meetings, I posit that the leadership team should be, and remain at, about eight people (six to ten is fine). The VPs meeting, by contrast, should grow as the company scales. At a company of one thousand employees, the VPs meeting often has fifteen attendees. At Microsoft, this same meeting is over 150 attendees, or so I've been told.

CEO OPEN OFFICE HOUR

The CEO open office hour (which I highly recommend) can be scheduled anytime in the day. Each manager should set aside one hour each week for an open office hour, during which anyone can come introduce an issue. This ensures that all employees feel that they can be heard but limits the amount of time required to a predictable level for the manager.

ALL-HANDS MEETING

On a cadence that varies between once a week and once a month, it is important to have a company-wide all-hands meeting where the results of the most recent leadership team meeting are shared. Follow the same format. As always, allow time for anyone in the company to bring up their own issues or to provide feedback.

For another perspective, Peter Reinhardt of Segment shares: "We use all-hands meetings for sharing across teams of what teams are accomplishing and working on, celebrating wins (reinforce our values), and offering recognition broadly…plus bringing in customers to talk."

COMPANY-WIDE SOCIAL EVENT

If you have a regular company social event (which I recommend), the internal meeting day is a logical day to have it, as this is the day when the majority of your team will be in the office. If you need some ideas for this event, check out chapter 18, "Company Culture."

QUARTERLY OFF-SITES

In addition to the weekly (or biweekly, once your company is efficient) meetings, once a quarter, all the department heads (at least) should take a day or two to do quarterly planning. There are many ways this quarterly planning meeting can look—for example, only the department heads, or the entire company if the company is small—but they're usually held off-site, hence the common name in the industry: quarterly off-sites. Here's the overview of what should be addressed at every quarterly off-site meeting:

- **The past:** Do a retrospective on the prior quarter.
  - How did we do against our overall company OKRs and KPIs?
  - How did we function as a team? (360-degree feedback)
- **The future:** Plan for the future quarter.
  - Refresh vision and values.
  - Dig into issues and proposed solutions.
    - Use the exercise shared in the "Issue Identification" section of chapter 16.
  - Set the company's new OKRs (which then will cascade to departments, teams, and individuals).
  - Refresh the company's KPIs (which then will cascade to departments, teams, and individuals).
- **Bonding:** Get to know and like each other as human beings.
  - Structured activities

- Collect superficial personal information from employees such as the neighborhood or town they live in, their partner's name, their kid's name, their pet's name, their favorite food, and what they do for fun (to generate more interesting personal conversations).
  - Play a game of If You Really Knew Me to foster empathy and connection among the team.
  - Offer peer feedback. Use the feedback exercise shared in the "Conflict Resolution" section of chapter 16.
- Unstructured activities
  - Drinks at the bar
  - Sports, crafts, etc.
  - Events where spouses are invited

Because you want your employees to have fun, I recommend scheduling these quarterly off-site meetings on a Thursday or Friday so that you can then offer an optional weekend unstructured event with spouses. Team members oftentimes would like to get to know one another, but they are waiting for you to organize the events that will allow them to do so.

With that overview in mind, let's look closer at what it means to evaluate vision, values, and OKRS.

VISION

To create the ten-year company vision, imagine it is ten years from now. You are the dominant company in the industry. Ask yourself:

- What industry do you dominate?
- Who is your customer? (This should be a real live human being, not a corporate entity.)
- What pain are you solving for the customer?
- What is unique about your solution that causes the customer to choose you over the competition?
- What asset (human or physical) do you control that makes it difficult for any competitor to copy your solution? In other words, what is your moat?

VALUES

There are many ways to define your company's values.

A simple one is to complete the following sentence: "The rest of you in the company can make all of the decisions from now on, as long as you…" This is appropriate when the company is small and values are entirely aspirational.

Another way is to acknowledge the culture that you already have. To do this, each leadership team member should pick one person in the company who is not on the leadership team and exhibits a value that they wish would be a universal behavior. Name the person and the behavior. Then select three to five such examples. This method is best used when the company already has a sizable team and existing culture.

OKRs

For your quarterly goals, or OKRs (objectives and key results), the target is three and three: three objectives, with three key results for each objective. Create these OKRs for the company, then for each department (based on the company OKRs), then for each team (based on the department OKRs), and then for each individual (based on the team OKRs).

(Warning: A common mistake is to create department OKRs without creating company-level OKRs. This leads to siloed fiefdoms that neither work together nor trust each other.)

The objective (O) answers the question, "Where do we want to go?" This objective should tell a compelling story, akin to the tagline of a Hollywood movie. It does not need to be measurable (ironically, it can be subjective). But it should be inspiring.

Key results (KRs) answer the question, "How do we know that we're getting there?" KRs should be objectively measurable.

Here are examples:

Objective: Massively grow revenues
Key results:

- Reach $500,000 in monthly recurring revenue.
- Hire ten additional sales development reps.
- Hire a sales operations person to project manage the sales team.

Company OKRs should be broad enough that they encompass the whole company; each department and team should feel that their work is contributing to at least one of the company's priorities. Here are some examples of typical company-level OKRs:

- Profits: Massively grow revenues while minimizing expense.
- Product: Delight our customers.
- People: Create a positive and transparent environment where we are all inspired to do our best work.

Forming Various Levels of OKRs

At the end of every quarter, gather the leadership team together and collaborate on the coming quarter's OKRs during the quarterly off-site meeting. I've found the process that gets the best results and most buy-in is to use structured brainstorming: Ask every member of your leadership team to separately write up what they think the global OKRs of the company should be. Then simply combine everyone's ideas into one document. You will see common themes and have a healthy debate about the company's priorities.

The key thing to keep in mind when forming OKRs is to ensure that they are clearly defined and measurable so a third-party could adjudicate whether they were completed.

Once your leadership team has come up with the company's OKRs, share them with the wider team and instruct each department head to perform the same process within their department and then at the individual level during one-on-ones. Keep in mind it is much better for people to come up with their own OKRs (that align with the company's) than to just hand them down. That way they feel personally invested and have buy-in.

The OKR creation process is usually a distracting one. Therefore, dedicate one admin week (or less if at all possible) to creating department, team, and individual OKRs. Do all the other required quarterly admin processes (last quarter's OKR debrief, performance management, etc.) during that same week.

Here is a potential timeline for OKR creation during admin week:

Day 1. In the leadership team meeting (with all department heads), set aside two hours to create company OKRs using structured brainstorming.

Day 2. Each department has a group meeting (two hours) to create department OKRs. The manager checks and approves all department OKRs by the end of the day.

Day 3. Each team has a group meeting (two hours) to create team OKRs. The department head checks and approves all team OKRs by the end of the day.

Day 4. Each subteam has a group meeting (two hours) to create subteam OKRs. The team head checks and approves all subteam OKRs by the end of the day.

Day 5. Each individual creates individual OKRs. The subteam head checks and approves all individual OKRs by the end of the day.

Day 6. At the leadership team meeting, the CEO checks and approves all OKRs. All OKRs are announced to the company at the all-hands meeting.

Tracking OKRs

Create a system to track OKRs. Either use a third-party tool (Perdoo, Lattice) or create a traffic-lighted (green, yellow, red) spreadsheet. The system should show, week by week, which OKRs are on track (green), slightly off track (yellow), and far off track (red). See the example spreadsheet on pages 127–128.

Prompt the leadership team to update the status of their OKRs (on track, lagging, poor) as part of the one-on-one process, and ask your managers to do likewise.

For all OKRs that are far off track, require that the DRI create a written description of the issue and solution to get back on track.

My CEO mentees tell me that this meetings system is the single most valuable part of the coaching experience for them, so implement it in your company too. You'll be glad you did. But remember, it's a complicated system at first. I highly recommend hiring an experienced COO full-time or a one-day-a-week CEO to come in and implement this system for you.

Group	Owner	Objective	KPI	8/29/18	9/5/18	9/12/18	9/19/18
Company	CEO	Company is aligned, efficient, and effective	Survey remote team for ideas and implement at least 3 things to improve remote inclusion	ON TRACK	ON TRACK	ON TRACK	
			Implement OKRs and KPIs company-wide	ON TRACK	ON TRACK	ON TRACK	
			Ship company values and brand platform	ON TRACK	ON TRACK	ON TRACK	
		Product X is fully ready to launch (sell)	Have at least 10 paying customers who are using Product X	POOR	POOR	POOR	
			Develop and ship top 3 uses cases	LAGGING	LAGGING	LAGGING	
			Create go-to-market plan (pricing, distribution, sales motion)	LAGGING	LAGGING	LAGGING	
		Massively grow revenues to be on a long-term track for IPO	Hire sales and customer success per $15M forecasting plan	LAGGING	ON TRACK	ON TRACK	
			Be on track for $15M by end of year	LAGGING	LAGGING	LAGGING	
			Lower annual churn to 15% (not including upsells)	POOR	POOR	POOR	

Group	Owner	Objective	KPI	8/29/18	9/5/18	9/12/18	9/19/18
Product	Head of product	Product X is fully ready to launch (sell)	Ship sales alerting/analytics for Product X	ON TRACK	ON TRACK	ON TRACK	ON TRACK
			Finish minimum 2 rounds of customer development to assure we're on track	LAGGING	LAGGING	LAGGING	LAGGING
			Complete go-to-market materials	ON TRACK	ON TRACK	ON TRACK	ON TRACK
		Increase customer retention/upsell	Ship Product B requirements (as defined by Q3 product roadmap)	LAGGING	LAGGING	ON TRACK	ON TRACK
			Ship Product A v2	ON TRACK	LAGGING	LAGGING	LAGGING
			Improve data per items on Q3 roadmap	ON TRACK	ON TRACK	ON TRACK	ON TRACK
		Build out a world-class product process and team	Deliver written product organization process	LAGGING	LAGGING	LAGGING	LAGGING
			Write out hiring plan and achieve it	POOR	POOR	POOR	POOR
			Never block engineering on product design; specs/design lead engineering kickoff by 3 weeks	LAGGING	LAGGING	LAGGING	LAGGING

Frequent, transparent feedback is critical for building a strong culture and a thriving business. Feedback is instrumental for building trust. Without trust, communication breaks down. Building a culture of feedback and transparency starts and ends with the founders.

RECEIVING

Receiving critical feedback in particular should be cherished. Your team members are in the trenches every day. They have knowledge about the company that you do not have. Only if you open the door to negative feedback will your team feel comfortable giving it. Think about it from the other side—it can be quite scary to criticize someone who has power over you. They might feel as if they're risking their job!

If you do not proactively collect feedback, you will quickly find that the following problems emerge:

- You will be in the dark about your company's problems. Ben Horowitz says that "a good culture is like the old RIP routing protocol: bad news travels fast, good news travels slow." If you react defensively every time your team members bring up an issue, they will soon stop bringing that valuable information to you, and you will crumble in your ivory tower.
- Operations will grind to a halt. When people aren't able to share things openly, communication breaks down. When communication breaks down, operations slow. This problem only gets worse as your company grows, and as it grows it becomes ever harder to change that culture.
- Your best talent will leave you. A players have no patience for defensiveness and amateurishness. If you aren't mature enough to listen to your people, face your problems, and work on fixing them, your A players will find the founders who are.

Therefore, if you are to receive real, honest feedback and improve—and keep your team communicating—*you* must make the effort to seek it out. Do so using the three *A*s:

- Ask for it. Make sure your team understands that giving you negative feedback will not be punished but cherished. It is important to explicitly say this to them, preferably in a one-on-one setting. When asking for feedback on the company in general, it is useful to ask, "If you were CEO, what would you change?" You can do this in person or through an anonymous survey. When asking for feedback about himself as a manager, Lachy Groom of Stripe asks, "What feedback are you afraid to give because you think it might hurt my feelings? Please tell me that."

- Appreciate it. Don't interrupt your team member. Don't give excuses. Your job is to listen and try your utmost to understand. Say thank you for the precious gift that you are receiving. Only once you understand the issue, you've repeated it back to them, and they know that you've understood their issues can you initiate a conversation about potential solutions.

- Act on it. Actions speak infinitely louder than words. If you have agreed with someone's negative feedback, work on changing the problem immediately. Do not let it fall through the cracks. Doing so will result in your team losing trust in your word and therefore losing motivation. Instead, create actual next actions (in GTD terminology—see chapter 3) on the issue. Only then will your team members feel confident that their voices are heard and safe enough to give you further feedback.

GIVING

When giving feedback, it is critical to use a two-way communication method (in person is best, video call is okay, audio call is least good). This is so that you can see the person's reaction. If they get defensive and angry, you will be able to see that and say, "I didn't intend to make you feel angry. My intent was to be helpful." This will hopefully mollify their anger.

If, on the other hand, you use a one-way communication method (email, text, or voicemail), then the recipient can easily become defensive and angry without you realizing it. And because you don't notice the anger, you won't be able to address it. Unaddressed, that anger will soon turn into resentment toward you. Therefore, do not use a one-way communication method (email, text, or voicemail) to give feedback, unless it is 100 percent positive. There is one exception to this rule: if you already know the person to be open, curious, and desirous of critical feedback.

Here is a template for providing good feedback, adapted from the book *Nonviolent Communication* by Marshall B. Rosenberg.

1. Ask for permission. Give the receiver a little heads-up of what's coming. It can be enough to say, "I have something to communicate to you. Is now a good time?"
2. State the trigger behavior or event (fact). Try to be factual ("When you are late to meetings…") as opposed to interpretive ("When you disrespect me…").
3. State how that trigger behavior makes you feel in terms of anger, sadness, and fear (feeling). This is perhaps the hardest part for many founders to do. Talking about your feelings might not be something you are used to, so it might be challenging at first. However, doing so is crucial for the other person to truly understand where you are coming from and to take your feedback to heart.
4. State the thoughts, opinions, and judgments (story) you have around this situation.
5. Make a request of what you would like to see. Try to frame it as positive action ("Do *x*") rather than a negative ("Don't do *y*").
6. Ask if the person accepts the feedback and the request. If yes, hold them accountable to doing it.

Giving and receiving frequent and transparent feedback may be painful at first. Often when companies start implementing this, it brings up a lot of underlying resentment and repressed issues. However, if you hang in there, you will find the amount and intensity of feedback diminishes substantially, and your team will be noticeably happier and more productive.

PART VI
PROCESSES

Inside your company's walls, you have your key personnel in place and functioning effectively, your data systems up and running, and information flowing easily from your managers to your team members and vice versa. The last piece of the puzzle, of course, is your dealings with the outside world—with investors, recruits, and customers. These processes—fundraising, recruiting, and sales—are all identical. They differ only in the contents of the exchange.

In fundraising, you are selling the company's equity and debt as a high-quality investment, and the investor is compensating you with capital. In recruiting, you are selling the company as a high-quality employment opportunity, and the new employee is giving you their time and effort as payment. In sales, you are selling your product as a high-quality solution, and the customer is giving you money as payment.

In each of these cases, someone is making the decision to invest in you or your company, whether with money or time. As such, you'll need to build trusting relationships with these decision makers in order to fundraise, recruit, or sell.

Peter Reinhardt of Segment correctly points out, "It is also a process of aligning a huge number of complex stakeholders to accomplish something together."

PICK A PARTNER, NOT A FIRM

When you raise money, you also get an investor. It's standard for firms to assign one partner to manage the relationship, but don't let this fall to chance. Make sure you get the partner who you believe will add value and be good to work with. Find out from other founders who at each firm is the good person to work with. Make sure they're going to be with the firm for the long term. Then approach them.

The introduction is a key part of the fundraising process, and you get only one chance at it. I recommend using the triangulation method.

When you want to be introduced to an investor, first find three to five people in your network who know that person. Then ask those three to five people each to send an email to the target investor, letting the target investor know how great they think you are and highly recommending meeting you. After receiving several such emails, the investor will proactively reach out to you. The investor has received recommendations before, but never three or more for the same person. The investor concludes that you and your company must be truly great and is already inclined to invest in you before even meeting you.

From your side, stack all the referrals in a short period of time (within a week). You are trying to achieve critical mass and have the referrals rise above the noise of other referrals. Stacking the referrals close together ensures that they rise above the noise.

It's important not to hand each referrer the same potential text to send onward. If they end up sending the same language, then the referrals are revealed to be orchestrated by you. Therefore, either give your referrers different suggested language or no suggestion at all.

TWO FUNDRAISING METHODS

There are two ways to raise money: the traditional method and the relationship method.

The traditional method is when you pitch an investment firm with your story, most often with a slide deck that describes the customer problem and your solution, market size, unit economics, financial projections, competition, team members, traction, go-to-market strategy, and so on. You might run through your presentation dozens of times before you find a spark of interest in either you or your company.

The relationship method is when you build a trusting, friendly relationship with an investor before ever discussing what your company does. This takes more time, but it dramatically increases the close rate. This works because no matter how rational we appear, we are most often guided by our emotional responses. We make instinctive, gut choices, and our rational brains do an excellent job of retrofitting logic over those choices.

The very first time you talk about your company, the investor will make a decision about whether they want to invest. If they do not yet like or trust you, then your company had better be optically perfect—and more often than not, it isn't. So the key is to wait to talk about your company until you are sure that the investor likes and trusts you personally. By then the investor will have a positive bias toward you and will be inclined to invest in your company, warts and all.

But how do you get the investor to like and trust you?

BUILD TRUST AND LIKE

Think about the people you like. Do you like people who just talk about themselves and show no interest in or curiosity about you and your life? Or do you like people who ask about you, listen attentively, and are genuinely curious about what makes you tick?

When meeting potential investors for the first time, ask them about themselves. Get genuinely curious about their lives, both at work and at home. Ask them lots of questions. Prove to them you're listening by saying, "I think I heard you say…" and then repeating back to them the highlights of what they said to you. When the meeting ends, write down as much information about the person as you remember.

At your next meeting with them, say, "The last time we talked, you said…" and again repeat the highlights. It is heartwarming when we find someone who cares enough about the details of our lives to remember them.

Also let them know what they have done that you appreciate. If nothing else, you can always appreciate the fact that they took the time to meet with you.

But how do you get a meeting in the first place without the explicit purpose of talking about your company? You can use the triangulation method, described above, but if you don't have enough mutual acquaintances, you can simply ask for it. Be explicit about your intent to build a relationship. Say something like "I only want to work with investors with whom I have a good relationship. So let's start with a coffee to get to know each other personally."

After the first meeting, ask for a second. Since the stated purpose is to build a relationship, the investor is likely to say yes. If you have truly allowed them to speak about themselves, they will have enjoyed the meeting and will look forward to another.

These meetings do not need to be long, nor do they need to be in person. A fifteen-minute phone call can be as effective as a one-hour meal if, after time has passed, you demonstrate genuine care and a memory for the details of their life. After two meetings like this, when you listen to them and reflect back what they say, they will trust and like you. Several more and they will love you. You'll know when the moment comes that they like and trust you. They will likely say it. If not, their body language will show it.

You can then proceed to talk about your company with the confidence that they are already inclined to invest. If you aren't good at reading body language, just wait. At some point, they will say something like (and this is an actual quote from an investor) "I really like you. I want to invest in you. Now tell me what your company does."

To summarize, the four keys are as follows:

- Ask them about their lives.
- Prove that you heard them by saying, "I think I heard you say…"
- Prove that you remember by saying at the next meeting, "The last time we talked you said…"
- Let them know what you appreciate about them.

If you do all four of these things, you will have created a bond, and you then have a willing investor.

When most CEOs hear of this method for the first time, they have a strong negative reaction. This method feels unnatural and goes against their instincts to close quickly. Later, once they have tried the method and it works like a charm, they become raving fans. My best advice, therefore, is to try it on a few prospective investors and see if it is more effective than the traditional approach.

STRENGTHEN THE RELATIONSHIP

Once you have met with someone a couple of times and demonstrated your memory and care for their lives, you have created a relationship. This is likely enough for them to like you. But why settle for just enough? To further strengthen the relationship, continue to be curious about them, and show them that you remember what they say. Three to five rounds of contact will solidify the relationship. Not every round of contact needs to be an in-person meeting—it can be enough to send a quick message.

Here is an example of a message of appreciation that comes from a managing partner at one of the most successful investment firms in the world:

Hey Matt,

Just wanted to drop a note of thanks. I really enjoyed our talk on Tuesday and brief ones since. Also greatly appreciate you treating me to lunch. Talk soon!

Bill

I feel honored that he took the time to appreciate me.

The following tip comes from Andy Bromberg, founding CEO of CoinList, who takes it a step further: "At the risk of giving up my secrets, I'd suggest handwritten thank-you notes. The response I get to my handwritten notes is incredible. People are floored. And often remember me as 'the handwritten note guy.'"

So make it a practice to regularly go through your contact list and send out messages of appreciation. You will be shocked by the massive goodwill that it generates. Andy suggests making this a formal process.

He says, "Every day I review all my interactions and send (or schedule) thank-yous as appropriate. It ensures I don't miss anyone and am prompt. And it takes literally a few minutes."

SELL YOURSELF, NOT YOUR COMPANY

Cliff Weitzman, CEO of Speechify, realized that it was key to sell himself and not his company. If he was able to do so, he would gain investors for life—investors who would follow him through every pivot and every company. So when Cliff realized that trust and like had been established, he shared the story of his life—using a method that his brother Tyler had discovered.

Tyler Weitzman, CEO of Black SMS, likes to research social situations. As an undergraduate at Stanford, he researched a method for conveying one's achievements (or bragging, if you prefer!) while remaining humble and relatable. Through countless interviews with master storytellers, Tyler determined the ultimate structure for telling one's story in a humble way:

- **Credit:** "It could not have happened without [name the others involved]."
- **Hard work:** "We had to put in so much to make it happen, for example, [describe the hard work]."
- **Vulnerability:** "It was most difficult for me when…"
- **Duty:** "We were driven by our dream to [noble motive]."
- **Gratitude:** "I am so proud and thankful that…"

I encourage you to tell your story to a friend using this exact structure. See what comes out. Ask your friend for her reaction. I think you will be amazed.

For an example of this method, see the acknowledgments section at the end of this book.

TIMING

There are milestones in a startup's life that, once achieved, make it significantly more likely that the company will eventually succeed. Each of these milestones, or inflection points, greatly reduces the company's risk and makes it much easier to raise money. Your company's value, then, does not rise in a linear fashion but in a stair-step pattern, as indicated in the chart.

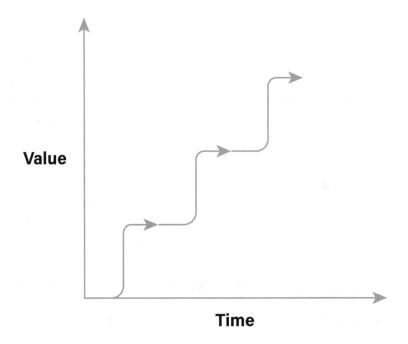

Here are some examples of inflection points:

- Hiring a capable engineering team
- Signing up your first three paying customers
- Exceeding $1 million in annual recurring revenue (ARR), which demonstrates product-market fit
- Hiring a capable sales team
- Exceeding $5 million in ARR, which demonstrates the effectiveness of your sales team
- Hiring senior managers for all departments

The best time to raise money is just after you've hit an inflection point. This is because your company has just increased in value but will not increase further until it hits the next milestone, which could be months away.

A SAFE and its cousin the convertible note are investments that are used when it is impractical to create a priced equity round, either because the amount raised is too small or you do not have an institutional investor to lead the round. Priced equity rounds usually incur large legal costs, often over $100,000, which the company invariably ends up paying for. SAFEs and notes are much less expensive, with legal fees often less than $10,000. Therefore, you should do a priced equity round only if the total money raised will exceed $2 million, and preferably exceeds $5 million.

SAFEs usually convert at a discount to the next priced equity round and can also have a valuation cap. I recommend always having a SAFE open, even after you do a priced round. Here is an example of what this might look like:

- When you start your company, you would raise your initial money of $2–5 million in a SAFE.
- When you hit product-market fit, you raise an additional $2–10 million in a Series A priced round and the SAFE converts into this round.
- You then immediately make available another SAFE. Continue to leave it available until you have raised another $5–10 million.
- Once you hit $5 million in ARR, you raise a Series B priced round of an additional $5–20 million and the second SAFE converts into this round.
- You then make available a third SAFE round and so on.

Institutional investors prefer to invest in priced equity rounds. But family offices, and even strategic investors who are not accustomed to leading priced rounds, are often very willing to participate in SAFEs, even as the company matures, as long as they have confidence that there will be another priced equity round. Therefore, there is little downside in always raising the first tranche of a round in a SAFE. This money extends your runway to reach the metrics required to raise the next priced equity round.

PRICED ROUNDS

BY ALEX MACCAW

At some point you will need to convert your SAFEs and do a proper priced round. This usually happens at the Series A but can sometimes happen at the seed. Since this involves a lot of custom terms and negotiation, it can be an expensive process in regard to both time and cash.

What often happens is that founders receive a bunch of term sheets with artificial timelines. Then they rush through the process and end up signing terms without understanding the long-term ramifications.

It is incredibly important to take your time and not make any mistakes here; they will come back to haunt you! Treat this process as irreversible. Take your time to go through every clause in the term sheet with your lawyers to fully understand each one.

Investors have a huge informational advantage over you. They sign these term sheets all the time. They're experts at controlling companies as minority shareholders. Often the tools they use are hidden in the "special provisions" set of clauses. While you may think these provisions innocuous at the time, they can be activated out of left field when you least expect it (like when you're selling your company).

Don't rely on your lawyers to highlight the dodgy terms. What they may consider standard, you may not. Pass your term sheets (scrubbed if necessary) by other founders and investors you trust for feedback. If you do discover unethical terms, blacklist that investor.

LEGAL EXPENSES

You will need a name-brand law firm to manage your priced rounds. They will only be too eager to help; this is one of their favorite ways to bill large amounts. But there is a technique to manage costs and time. If you let them bill however they want to, the end result could easily be over $100,000 for a Series A investment. If you manage them aggressively, however, you can get that bill down to $15,000 or less. This is important because the company is often required to pay for both their own counsel and that of the investor if the bill exceeds a certain amount (usually $25,000).

A typical investment happens like this:

1. Lawyers call each other to discuss the terms. They disagree on a point.
2. The company lawyer calls the company decision maker for guidance. (For every email written or voicemail left, the lawyer charges for fifteen minutes minimum but usually one hour.)
3. The company decision maker responds to the company lawyer (another billable hour).
4. The company lawyer reaches out to the investor lawyer (another billable one to two hours).
5. The investor lawyer then reaches out to the investor decision maker on this same issue (another billable one to two hours).
6. The investor lawyer responds to the decision maker lawyer (another billable one to two hours).
7. This continues back and forth, racking up billable hours, until every detail is agreed on. The process takes forty-five to sixty days to get final documents, and the legal bill is often over $100,000 from each side.

But there is another way. It results in final documents in less than one week and legal bills of less than $15,000 from each side.

Investors must pay for legal bills out of their management fee income. This income would otherwise go into their individual pockets, so investors do not like to pay for legal fees (even their own). They would much prefer to give the company more money (which comes out of the fund's investment capital) and have the company pay for the investors' lawyers. Make this accommodation for investors. Require only that the investor support you in enforcing rules of behavior on their lawyers. And those rules are as follows:

- Once the basic terms of investment are agreed on (in a term sheet), then a four- to eight-hour meeting (or call) is scheduled. (This meeting may last only two to three hours, but it is very important that enough time be blocked off to allow it to run longer if necessary.) The following attendees are required:

- ○ Decision maker from the company
- ○ Decision maker from the lead investor
- ○ Lawyer for the company
- ○ Lawyer for the lead investor

- If any of these four people cannot make the meeting (or call), then the meeting is rescheduled.

- The lawyer for one side prepares the first draft of the investment documents. The lawyer for the other side responds with written comments before the meeting or call. There is no other contact between the lawyers.

- At the meeting, everyone reviews the documents from beginning to end, paragraph by paragraph, and addresses all the written comments. Lawyers are not allowed to speak except to advise their client on the meaning of the paragraph being reviewed. The negotiation is between decision makers at the company (such as the CEO) and the lead investor directly. The decision makers go through every point until they have reached agreement on all of them. As each point is agreed on, the lawyers then in real time agree on the wording that best reflects the business agreement that was just made.

- The lawyer who wrote the base document then writes up the final language. The other lawyer confirms that this language is exactly what they had agreed on during the meeting. The documents are then final.

In this process, the lawyer for the company can bill for no more than the following time:

4 hours	Write up base documents
1 hour	Read comments before the big meeting
8 hours	Attend the big meeting
4 hours	Write up final language
17 hours	**@ $800 per hour = $13,600**

In this process, the lawyer for the investor can bill for no more than the following time:

4 hours	Write comments on the base documents
8 hours	Attend the big meeting
2 hours	Read the final language
14 hours	**@ $800 per hour = $11,200**

This same technique can be used for the creation of any negotiated legal documents (e.g., contract for a large sale).

CAP TABLE

There are several other topics to consider regarding the cap table: voting, liquidity, Carta, 409A, and option pools.

VOTING

Mark Zuckerberg retains total control of Facebook even though he owns only a minority of its shares. Why? Because the shares he owns come with extra votes. Now that this structure has been accepted by investors, there is little reason not to set it up in your own company. And the easiest time to do this is prior to having equity investors. Ask your lawyers to set up "FF shares with ten times or twenty times voting rights" prior to investors being on the cap table (SAFEs are fine).

LIQUIDITY

In addition, FF shares allow founders to get liquidity at each priced round without raising the fair market valuation of the options granted to other team members. This allows founders to continue to pay themselves low salaries (excellent optics within the company) but still get enough liquidity to not worry about committing themselves to the company for the long term. Again, these should be created prior to having equity investors.

CARTA (FORMERLY ESHARES)

Managing stock certificates is painful for both investors and the company. Avoid the hassle by using an electronic system like Carta from day one. It costs far less than paying your law firm's paralegal $300 an hour to answer every question your investors have about their ownership. Carta provides instant access to that information for your investors, who likely already have most of their portfolio on Carta. And the attached 409A valuation service costs about a quarter of what other independent 409A services charge.

409A

You will need to do a valuation of your common stock to determine the correct exercise price of any options that you issue. This is a 409A (the IRS code) valuation and must be done *before* issuing the options. You will need to update this 409A valuation yearly or when you experience a change in your company's value (new financing, major customer addition, etc.).

OPTION POOLS

When fundraising for a priced equity round, know that investors will want to see enough unissued options (option pool) remaining that there will be a 10–20 percent unallocated option pool *after* the equity investment. This fact often catches founders by surprise. When the venture firm offers $4 million on a post-money valuation of $20 million, the founders think that they have been diluted by 20 percent. But this same offer will almost always require that a large option pool be created before the equity comes in. This post-money option pool plus the new equity therefore represents a 40 percent dilution to the existing shareholders. There isn't much you can do about this. Just be aware of it.

Fundraising is a critical part of a tech company's growth, so embrace the process, be aware of potential pitfalls, and don't be afraid to experiment.

When recruiting, the goal is to find great people and attract them to your company. Since this is so important, you could rationalize throwing lots and lots of time at this problem, and that is what most growing companies do. Unfortunately this time-suck will grind most of your other functions to a halt.

The key is efficiency. And to be efficient, you must spend as little time as possible with the candidates you don't hire (quick evaluation) and as much time as possible with the candidates you want to and do hire (building a relationship and onboarding/training). Remember that each minute you spend with a candidate you don't hire is a minute that you aren't spending with the candidate you want to hire.

Of all the recruiting systems I have seen, the best is described in *Who* by Geoff Smart and Randy Street. Here's a brief look at the main points of *Who*.

WHO RECRUITING PROCESS

The goal of the *Who* recruiting process is to hire only A players. These are the right superstars who can do the job you need done while fitting in with the culture of your company. The *Who* methodology involves creating a scorecard and specific processes for sourcing, selecting, and selling candidates to join your company. In this section, we'll look at each of these steps in turn, as well as how to implement this system and legal issues to be aware of when hiring.

SCORECARD

The scorecard is a document created by the hiring manager that describes exactly what they want a person to accomplish in a specific role. The scorecard includes a mission, outcomes, and competencies that define the job.

- The mission describes the business problem and its solution. For example, "The operations lead will create and manage a world-class department that will support every team member by providing the environment, information, tools, training, and habits they need to succeed in their role and make the company a massive success."

- The outcomes are *what* the person must get done. There should be three to eight outcomes (target is five) ranked by order of importance. They should be measurable and have an accomplish-by date. For example, "Turn every team member into a ninja user of our internal tools (Asana, Salesforece, Notion) and methodologies (GTD, Inbox Zero, management by objectives, active listening) by October 31."
- The competencies are the traits or habits that are required to succeed in the role and fit in at the company. They are the *how*—the behaviors that someone must exhibit in order to achieve the outcomes. Here are some examples:
  - Organized: Follows the GTD method and stays well aware of all to-dos and events
  - Innovative: Seeks to make process improvements to make their role and the team more efficient going forward
  - Collaborative: Reaches out to peers and cooperates with managers to establish an overall collaborative environment
  - Persuasive: Is able to convince others to pursue a course of action
  - Coachable: Wants to improve and is open to feedback and acts on that feedback

After the scorecard is created, it is compared with the company and department roadmaps and the scorecards of other employees whom the person will interface with. This is done to ensure alignment (i.e., every employee has a set of outcomes that support the company's strategy and competencies that support the outcomes and culture), and then the scorecard is shared with relevant team members, including peers and recruiters. Creating a good scorecard will help you find A players who can do the job that is needed today and have the flexibility and adaptability for what their role may become tomorrow.

SOURCE

All hiring managers should always be systematically sourcing—that is, identifying the *who* before a new hire is needed. There are three sources for finding candidates:

- Referrals from your network
- Recruiters
- Researchers

Referrals from your personal and professional networks are by far the most effective. Use this process for sourcing such referrals:

1. Create a list of the ten most talented people you know.
2. Commit to speaking to at least one of them each week for the next ten weeks, asking them, "Who are the three most talented people you know?"
3. Continue to build your list and continue to talk with at least one person per week.
4. Document everything in your company's applicant tracking system (ATS).

Other strategies for sourcing from your network include hosting a sourcing party and offering referral bonuses. To host a sourcing party, schedule it, gather the team in one room, and then ask all attendees to reach out to as many candidates in their network as possible. Gamify the process. Make it fun. Give a prize to whomever reaches out to the most people (or whatever other metric you want to use).

Recruiters are not as effective as your own network. To be effective at all, recruiters need to know and understand your company and product. It is pointless to engage recruiters unless you bring them in, give them full access to your scorecards, and share every detail of your reaction to the candidates they propose.

Researchers are people who research networks and generate names but do not reach out directly to candidates.

SELECT

The selection process is when you conduct structured interviews that rate candidates against the scorecard you've created. To be a great interviewer, you must get out of the habit of passively witnessing how somebody acts during interviews. Instead, use the interviews to collect facts and data about how the candidate has performed in the past. There are four types of interviews to conduct:

- Screening interview
- Topgrading interview
- Focused interview
- Reference interview

The goal of the screening interview is to eliminate people who are inappropriate for the position as soon as possible. This interview is conducted by phone and should not last more than thirty minutes. Schedule the call for fifteen minutes, then extend it to thirty minutes during the call only if the candidate appears to be excellent.

The hiring manager will assign someone to conduct the first screen. If the candidate passes, the hiring manager will do the second screen.

Here's a sample script for the screening interview:

1. "Thanks for taking the time to talk to me. I'd like to spend the first ten minutes of our call getting to know you. After that, I'm happy to answer any questions you have about us. Sound good?"
2. "What are your career goals?"
   a. If the candidate's goals sound like an echo of your company's website or they don't have any, screen them out.
3. "What are you really good at professionally?"
   a. Push the candidate to give you eight to twelve positives, with examples, so that you can build a complete picture of their capabilities. You are listening for strengths that match the scorecard.
4. "What are you not good at or not interested in doing professionally?"
   a. Push the candidate for real weaknesses, five to eight of them. If they don't respond thoroughly, call them out on it. If they still don't, then say, "If you advance to the next step in our process, we will ask for your help in setting up reference calls with your bosses, peers, and subordinates. What do you think they will say are some things that you are not good at or not interested in?"

5. "Who were your last three bosses, and how will they each rate your performance on a 0–10 scale when we talk to them?"
   a. Press for details of why each person would give them such a rating. We are looking for consistent 8s to 10s. A 6 is actually a 2. But ask why it's a 6.
6. Throughout the interview, get curious. Ask follow-up questions that start with "What," "How," and "Tell me more."
   a. "What do you mean?"
   b. "What is an example of that?"
   c. "How did you do that?"
   d. "How did that feel?"

If you can't definitively say, "This is an A player," then hit the gong. It is better to miss out on an A player than to waste many precious hours on a borderline case that turns out to be a B or C player. If you weed harshly, you will be able to spend more time with candidates who are known A players. End the call at the scheduled time (fifteen minutes, hopefully). Within twenty-four hours, inform the candidate that you appreciated their time but you will not be moving forward with them: "Thank you for taking the time to interview with us. We do not feel that our needs for this role match your strengths. That being said, we will be hiring for many more roles in the future, and we hope to be able to reach back out to you again." While it may feel difficult to say no to people, it is disrespectful to let them linger. The vast majority of people prefer a quick no to a slow one, or worse yet, no response at all.

If you think the candidate is an A player, let them know that you think they're great and that you are open to extending this phone interview to get to know them more and answer their questions about the job and the company.

At the end of the phone interview, let the candidate know that you would like to immediately schedule the next interview (which is either the second phone interview or the on-site interviews).

THE DAY OF ON-SITE INTERVIEWS

For the on-site interviews, schedule them back-to-back (with some break time in between) with all the needed decision makers, followed by a decision meeting at the end of the day attended by all interviewers. The goal is to get all needed buy-in for a yes or no decision in one day of interviews.

This day of on-site interviews will include the topgrading interview and several focused interviews. The day's schedule will look something like this:

8:30–9:00 a.m.	Interview team meeting: The hiring manager explains what's going to happen today and reviews the scorecard, the candidate's résumé, the notes from the screening interviews, and everyone's roles and responsibilities for the day.
8:45–9:00 a.m.	A team member (host) greets the candidate and orients them to the day ahead.
9:00–11:00 a.m.	Topgrading interview (1–2 hours)
11:00 a.m.–noon	Focused interview
Noon–1:00 p.m.	Lunch with _____
1:00–4:00 p.m.	Focused interviews
4:00–4:15 p.m.	The host thanks the candidate and explains next steps.
4:15–5:00 p.m.	Decision meeting: The interview team meets to rate the scorecard. The hiring manager makes a yes or no decision to conduct reference calls or terminate the process.

TOPGRADING INTERVIEW

The goal of the topgrading interview is to understand the candidate's story and patterns. These stories and patterns are predictive of the candidate's future performance. Start from the beginning and move forward chronologically. This interview should take about two hours (three hours for a CEO; one hour for an entry-level position). It is worth the time. For every hour you spend topgrading a candidate, you'll save hundreds of hours not dealing with B or C players.

The hiring manager should conduct the topgrading interview, along with a colleague who wants to learn the method by observing.

At the beginning of the interview, set expectations by saying:

"Thank you for visiting us today. We are going to do a chronological interview and walk through each job you've had. For each job, I am going to ask you five core questions:

1. What were you hired to do?
2. What accomplishments are you most proud of?
3. What were some low points during that job?
4. Who were the people you worked with?
5. Why did you leave that job?

At the end of the interview, we will discuss your career goals and aspirations, and you can ask me questions about us.

Eighty percent of the process will take place in this room, but if we mutually decide to move forward, we will conduct reference calls to complete the process.

Finally, while this sounds lengthy, it will go remarkably fast. It is my job to guide the pace of the discussion. Sometimes I will ask you to go into more depth; other times I will ask that we move on to the next topic. I'll try to make sure that we leave plenty of time to cover your most recent and therefore most relevant jobs.

Any questions before we begin?"

Here are additional details about the questions you should ask for each job the candidate had.

1. "What were you hired to do?" You are trying to create a picture of what their scorecard was, if they had one. What were their mission and key outcomes (or OKRs)?
2. "What accomplishments are you most proud of?" Hopefully these accomplishments will match the outcomes described in the first question.
3. "What were some low points during that job?" Do not let the candidate off the hook. Reframe the question over and over again until you get real answers.
4. "Who were the people you worked with?" Specifically:
   a. "What was your boss's name, and how do you spell that? What was it like working with them? What will they tell me were your biggest strengths and areas for improvement?" Follow the script exactly. By letting the candidate know that you will be contacting these references, the candidate will become much more truthful. This is

the most important question that you ask during the topgrading interview, as it gives us the information needed to do the reference interviews. For the most recent or significant job, also ask:

b. "Who were your peers on the team, and how do you spell their names?"

c. "Who were the members of your team, and how do you spell their names?" Again, these are critical questions that will enable the reference interviews.

d. "How would you rate the team you inherited on an A, B, and C scale? What changes did you make? Did you hire anybody? Fire anybody? How would you rate the team when you left it on an A, B, and C scale?" Does the candidate accept the hand they have been dealt, or do they make changes to get a better hand? To get more information, you can also ask, "When we speak with members of your team, what will they say are your biggest strengths and weaknesses as a manager?"

5. "Why did you leave that job?" Was the candidate promoted, recruited, or fired? Get very curious about why.

To conduct this interview well, know that you will have to do these things:

- Interrupt. Do so tactfully. But do not let a candidate ramble. Doing so will only hurt their chances of success, because it will chew up valuable time without conveying important information. Expect to interrupt the candidate once every three to four minutes. The proper way to interrupt someone is to be positive and use reflective listening: For example, you say, "Wow! It sounds like that pig farm next to the corporate office smelled horrible!" The candidate says, "Yes." Then you immediately say, "You were telling me earlier about launching that email campaign. I'd love to hear what that was like. How well did it go?"

- Ask about the three *P*s. Use the three *P*s (performance, plan, and peers) to clarify how valuable an accomplishment was in context.

  ○ "How did your performance compare to the previous year's performance?"

- ◦ "How did your performance compare to the plan?"
- ◦ "How did your performance compare to that of your peers?"
- Determine push versus pull. People who perform well are generally pulled to greater opportunities. For each job change, determine if it was a push or a pull.
  - ◦ Push: "It was mutual." "It was time for me to leave."
  - ◦ Pull: "My biggest client hired me." "My old boss recruited me to a bigger job."
- Paint a picture. You'll know that you understand what a candidate is saying when you can see a picture of it in your mind. Put yourself in their shoes.
- Stop at the stop signs. If you see or hear inconsistencies, the candidate may be telling an untruth. If this happens, get curious and dig deeper. Think of yourself as a biographer (positive), not an investigative journalist (negative).

Focused Interviews

The focused interviews provide a chance to involve other team members and get more specific information about the candidate. These interviews are focused on the outcomes (skills) and competencies (culture fit) on the scorecard. Team members should get curious after every answer by using the "What? How? Tell me more" framework. Have three team members (not the hiring manager) each conduct a fifty-minute focused interview. Split the outcomes and competencies from the scorecard up into three sections, allowing each interviewer to focus on one section (one-third of the outcomes and one-third of the competencies).

Here's a sample script:

1. "The purpose of this interview is to talk about [the outcome and competency to be reviewed]."
2. "What are your biggest accomplishments in this area during your career?"
3. "What are your insights into your biggest mistakes and lessons learned in this area?"

At the end of the day of on-site interviews, the entire interview team gathers for the decision meeting. All interview team members submit their comments about the candidates in writing in the ATS and then declare their positions on each candidate.

Only choose candidates whose skill (what they can do) and will (what they want to do) match the scorecard. This is their skill-will profile. For each item on the scorecard, rate the candidate's skill-will. Only rate people an A in whom you have a greater than 90 percent confidence that they can and will meet all outcomes and competencies.

Here are some red flags to watch out for during the interview process that signal problems:

- Candidate does not mention past failures.
- Candidate exaggerates answers.
- Candidate takes credit for the work of others.
- Candidate speaks poorly of past bosses.
- Candidate cannot explain job moves.
- Candidate's family doesn't want them to take this job.
- For managerial hires, candidate has never had to hire or fire anybody.
- Candidate is more interested in compensation and title than in the job itself and the company.
- Candidate tries too hard to look like an expert.
- Candidate is not curious about us or others. (Candidate is self-absorbed.)

Follow these steps to the selection process:

1. Update all the scorecards.
2. Rate each candidate.
3. If you have no As, restart the process.
4. If you have one A, make the candidate an offer pending reference interviews.
5. If you have several As, rank them and make an offer pending reference interviews to the best A among them. Try to find another role at the company for the other As.

Do not skip the reference checks! The reference interviews are where you learn the truth about the candidate. These interviews give you by far the most accurate picture of the candidate's future performance. There are three steps:

1. Pick the right references—bosses, peers, and subordinates (sometimes two to three levels down). Do not use the reference list that the candidate gave you.
2. Ask the candidate to contact the references you choose and set up the calls.
3. The hiring manager conducts at least two (but preferably four) reference interviews, and other team members do at least one (but preferably three) for a total of at least three (but preferably seven).

Here's a sample script:

1. "In what context did you work with the person?"
2. "What were the person's biggest strengths?" Get curious by using the "What? How? Tell me more" framework.
3. "What were the person's biggest areas for improvement back then?" It is very important to say *back then*. This liberates people to talk about real weaknesses, assuming that the candidate has improved them by now. (In reality, past performance is an indicator of future performance.)
4. "How would you rate their overall performance in that job on a scale of 0–10? What about their performance causes you to give that rating?"
5. "The person mentioned that they struggled with _____ in that job. Can you please tell me more about that?"

People do not like to give negative references, so listen for cues. Faint or qualified praise is damning, as is hesitation.

Danny An, founder of TrustToken, says, "When asking for weaknesses or areas of improvements during interviews and reference calls, people answer more freely if you say, 'People shouldn't do the majority of things and should focus on areas where they can use their strengths. Understanding weaknesses demonstrates self-awareness.'"

SELL

Your decision to hire the candidate is only one part of the equation. The next and even more critical part is selling the candidate on joining your company.

The key is to put yourself in the candidate's shoes. Find out what they care about. And then care about it yourself. These are the things most people tend to care about:

- Fit. Share the company roadmap, department roadmap, and their individual roadmap. Show how where they want to go is a match for where the company is going.
- Family. Ask, "What can we do to make this change as easy as possible for your family?" Ask about their family. Get to know their names, ages, and so on. Ask what concerns and needs their family members have and meet those needs. Ideally, meet their family in person (or, at a minimum, speak to their spouse on the phone), discover their needs directly, and meet those needs.
- Freedom. "At Company X, we collaboratively set company, department, and individual OKRs at the beginning of each quarter. Your individual OKRs mean that I will not micromanage you. In our regular one-on-one meetings, I will simply ask you to update me on your progress toward your OKRs and offer you support whenever you run into obstacles. I encourage you to talk to my team to see what I am like to work with."
- Fun. "Here is what we do for fun at the company."
- Fortune. "If you accomplish your objectives, and we as a company accomplish ours, you will likely make [amount] over the next five to ten years."

Selling happens throughout the recruiting process. Here are key moments to put yourself in a candidate's shoes and address the issues above:

- When you source
- When you interview
- The time between your verbal offer and the candidate's acceptance (reach out to them repeatedly during this time!)

- The time between the candidate's acceptance and their first day (yes, they still aren't really here yet; keep reaching out to them!)
- The new hire's first one hundred days on the job (yes, they are still evaluating; keep addressing the things that they care about!)

Be persistent. Too many candidates are lost because they feel abandoned once they are given an offer or arrive at the company.

IMPLEMENTATION

Here are the steps to implementing this recruiting system:

1. Announce it to the company.
2. Train all hiring managers and interviewers.
3. Implement the schedule and process. Enter the process and questions in the ATS.
4. Put "Source one great candidate" on everyone's quarterly scorecard (i.e., OKRs).

LEGAL

Don't discriminate. Hire people on one criteria only: whether they are likely to perform the job. Here are some things to keep in mind:

- Relevance. Defining the outcomes and competencies will ensure that you are judging on relevant criteria.
- Standardization. Having a standard process ensures fairness across all groups.
- Nondiscriminatory language. Do not use derogatory language toward anyone, ever.
- No illegal questions. Do not ask anything related to marital status, intention to have children, pregnancy, date or place of birth, medical condition, race or ethnicity, sexual orientation, or physical or mental handicaps.

That's a good at-a-glance summary of the system. For more detail, please read *Who* by Geoff Smart and Randy Street.

After years in the industry, I have a few additional recommendations, starting with what to do before recruiting and on through when you're selling, building a relationship, speed, compensation, making the offer, onboarding, and if eventually needed, firing.

BEFORE RECRUITING

As the hiring manager, write out a ninety-day roadmap for the position you need to fill. This roadmap is different from the scorecard in that it includes all the goals that the new team member will be expected to hit within the first ninety days of joining. This is critical for successful onboarding. During the interview process, share this roadmap with the candidate to make sure that they are excited about these goals.

SELLING

The best candidates will get offers from other companies. So you need to not only evaluate but also sell from the very beginning.

BUILDING A RELATIONSHIP

Just as in fundraising, building a relationship with a recruit will vastly increase the likelihood that they will want to join your company. The best candidates can work anywhere. Make sure that they want to work with you.

Do this by using the same techniques mentioned earlier. Ask the candidate about themselves, reflect back what they say, and remember what they said the next time you meet with them. If you have already used this method during your initial fundraising, you will know how effective it is.

SPEED

There is another key variable to making the recruit want to accept your offer: speed! A recruit wants to feel loved. The easiest way to accomplish that is to have a fast process from start to finish. Each day of delay sends the message "We don't have conviction about you."

If you doubt whether this really exists, just recall when you raised money. Which investors were the most compelling for you—the ones who responded and decided quickly, or the ones who lingered in their decision process for weeks or months? Benchmark and Sequoia are famous for making investment offers within days (and sometimes hours) of meeting a company that they are excited about.

The offer is always pending due diligence, so there is plenty of time after the fact to discover critical information. In recruiting, you would make an offer to the candidate "pending reference interviews." Here's what a streamlined process looks like:

1. You contact a candidate and schedule a short phone interview.
2. At the phone interview, the candidate appears to be an A player.
3. You immediately schedule a full-day, on-site interview to meet with all the needed interviewers. This is easily done because you already follow a calendar cadence, and so all needed interviewers have scheduled to be at the office on recruiting day, ready to interview. (Using this method, you can have several candidates for on-site interviews on the same day.)
   a. At the end of that day, the interview team convenes and makes a decision.
   b. If "yes," you reach out to the candidate that evening and say, "We love you. We want you to work at our company. We'd like to make you an offer pending reference interviews."
   c. You have a verbal discussion about what a successful offer would look like. You ask them to complete this phrase: "I would join your company as long as _____."
   d. You address each request. If all are doable, you move on to the next stage.
4. You conduct the reference interviews.
5. If those are positive, you reach back out to the candidate: "The reference interviews were great. We'd like for you to join our company. If we make you the following offer (explain every detail of the offer including benefits, etc.), would you accept?" Go back and forth until you have a verbal agreement.
6. You invite the candidate in for an "offer ceremony," wherein you make them the offer and they accept. (There is more detail on the offer process below.)

This process can take as little as two weeks from first contact to accepted offer. If your offer process becomes that fast, your acceptance rate from top candidates will start to resemble that of Benchmark and Sequoia.

Of course, because your acceptance rate will be so high, you can then afford to become incredibly picky and choose only the best of the best.

COMPENSATION

How much compensation do you offer new team members? How much cash and equity?

Here's my preferred method for setting these benefits:

1. Discover the market compensation for the position (role and seniority). There are plenty of online compensation studies that show this. Market compensation is whatever a big company (Microsoft, Facebook, Google) is paying for this position.
2. Discover the amount of cash that the new team member would need to live comfortably (housing, food, transportation, child expenses, etc.).

It is up to the startup to match the market compensation level, not in cash as the larger companies do, but rather in a much lesser amount of cash (no less than the amount needed to live comfortably), plus equity to bridge the difference.

Here is an example to show how the equity portion is calculated. Let's say the position is a level 3 engineer who is paid $300,000 in total compensation at Google. The team member requires $120,000 in cash to live comfortably and wants to invest the remainder in startup equity. The amount of equity is calculated by taking the difference between market and cash ($300,000 − $120,000 = $180,000) and multiplying it by four years ($180,000 × 4 = $720,000). This amount is then divided by a factor somewhere between 1 and 2, which represents a very conservative estimate of the increase in value of the equity over four years. A factor of 1 represents no expected increase in value. A factor of 2 represents a two-times expected increase in value. If a factor of 1.5 were used (which is the most common factor used), the final amount would be $720,000 ÷ 1.5 =

$480,000. So grant this amount in options, however much equity it purchases at the company's current valuation. The options vest over four years.

I prefer to then make an offer that allows the new team member to choose how much they want to invest in the startup equity at three different levels. The lowest cash level would be the level needed to live comfortably.

Here's an example in which the company is currently worth $50 million. The company will likely need to do another major round of financing along with option pool refresh before it gets to maturity, which is an expected 50 percent dilution to the current cap table. A $1 billion eventual value of the company would result in a ten-times increase in value of the equity. (A twenty-times increase in the company value multiplied by 50 percent dilution equals a ten-times increase in equity value.)

The three options would be as follows:

	Annual Cash	Equity Worth	Expected Value at $1 Billion Company Valuation
1	$120,000	$480,000	$4,800,000
2	$140,000	$426,666	$4,266,666
3	$160,000	$361,333	$3,613,333

The hope is that the new team member believes so fully in the company (and the power of the asymmetric bet) that they choose one of the two higher equity offers. This equity is thus an investment that the team member is making in the company. And with a huge advantage: the investment is made with pretax dollars, which doubles its purchasing power.

MAKING THE OFFER

Before making an offer, it is critical to know that the candidate will accept. Once you have the offer prepared, contact the candidate and ask them to complete the following sentence: "I will join the company as long as…"

They then should state all their requirements. If you are willing to provide each of these, then you are going to have a successful hire. If there is one that you cannot provide, discuss it with the candidate to see if there is some alternative that you both can accept.

Once this process is complete, then ask the candidate, "If we were to make you the following offer (state the offer in full detail, including cash, equity, benefits, etc.), would you accept?"

If the candidate says yes, then make the offer. If you skip this step and simply make the offer, then it is very common for the candidate to ask for a few more things after the fact (signing bonus, moving expenses, etc.). You will then be in the awkward position of either having to give these (and thereby allowing a political culture to begin) or starting the relationship on a negative note by saying no. It is far better to get the candidate to pre-agree in full detail before you make the offer. Then the relationship begins with a resoundingly positive "Yes! Thank you! I'm so excited!"

The granting and accepting of a job offer is a very emotional moment for a person. Making a big deal out of it is a good thing. Make a ceremony out of it. Invite the candidate to receive the offer in person. Create a ritual out of this process. Here are some possibilities:

- Hand the written offer to the candidate with two hands and a ceremonial bow.
- Give company schwag.
- Give hugs and high fives.

Whatever you do, make it fun and memorable.

ONBOARDING

Most companies spend extraordinary resources of time, money, and equity to bring on a new team member, and then almost entirely drop the ball on quickly getting that team member onboarded and up to speed on how the company works so that they can begin making a full contribution. Don't make this mistake! Give onboarding even more attention, time, and energy than you give to recruiting. After all, many of the people you are spending time with during recruiting will not become team members, whereas 100 percent of the people you spend time with during onboarding are already team members. Focus your energy there!

Write a checklist of all the information a team member would need to be fully effective. Write all this information down, and make a video of it. Share this checklist, the written and video information, and the ninety-day roadmap with each new team member as early as you can, even before they start.

On their first day at the office, have them come in two hours after the normal start of the workday so that plenty of people are there to greet the new team member. Assign each new team member a buddy with whom they'll check in each day for fifteen minutes for the first two weeks. These fifteen minutes are for the new team member to ask questions that arise and for the buddy to ensure that the new team member is actually going through the checklist.

The key thing to remember in onboarding is to give it just as much, if not more, time than the recruiting process. This is worth repeating: many of the people in the recruiting process will never work at the company, while everybody in the onboarding process will.

FIRING WELL

Inevitably some team members will not perform even with excellent onboarding, roadmap creation, feedback, and so on. When that happens, the chance that they will perform again in the future is very low, and the other team members will know, even more deeply than you do, that this person is not performing. Allowing this nonperformance will be a morale killer for the rest of the team, in addition to a financial drain that the company cannot afford. Therefore, you cannot allow it to continue. For the health of the company, you must let this person go. The expedient thing to do is to let the person go immediately. However, if you do not have written documentation of why you are firing someone, they can initiate a wrongful termination lawsuit against the company. These lawsuits are rarely successful, but they are distracting to respond to.

If you want to minimize the chance of one of these lawsuits occurring, then create written documentation. A secondary benefit of this documentation is that there is a small chance that the person will begin to perform. Here are the steps:

1. Create a written performance improvement plan (PIP) that states objective milestones and dates over a seven-, thirty-, sixty-, and ninety-day period.
2. Meet weekly to check progress against the written milestones.
3. At thirty days, if the team member hasn't hit one of the milestones, then you let them go.
4. At sixty days, the same.
5. And at ninety days, the same.

If, at any of these stages, the team member does not hit a milestone and you do not fire them, then you have completely invalidated the value of the written document, because you have established a provable pattern that the written document was not meaningful.

Again, know that there is a very low chance that the person will perform. If your team is very small (fewer than ten people), I recommend simply letting the person go without the PIP. The cost of demotivating the team is far greater than that of the lawsuit.

When you do fire someone, put yourself in their shoes. It is a devastating event emotionally. And it is a real setback financially. Your team will also be watching closely to see how you treat ex-employees; a vindictive attitude will make everyone feel unsafe!

Put real effort into helping the person find their next job, and quickly. Offer them a severance package that gives them enough time to realistically find another job and have the pay begin. This is one month minimum, but more realistically two to three months. And then help them find work within that time frame.

Because you value transparency, make an announcement to the company about the person's departure, or allow the person to do it themselves. When you make the announcement, praise the person's contributions to the company, and take ownership yourself for the fact that you weren't able to match their skills to the company's needs. Do not blame or criticize the person. Instead, take responsibility for the situation.

It is highly likely that you will be feeling anger toward this person. You will clearly value the rest of your team much more highly than this person. You will not want to give them an extra penny beyond what is required by law (two weeks). You will want to save those resources for the team members who remain and are performing.

Feel this anger, and then let it pass. Recognize that you have responsibility here. Your recruiting, training, and managing (or lack thereof) helped create this situation. It is your responsibility to help the person find a job and a company that is a better fit. If you want to save your company's resources, then help that person find that job more quickly. And then look at your recruiting, training, and managing processes, and ask yourself, "What can I do to make sure this doesn't happen again?"

If you do this, not only will you be doing the right thing and taking responsibility for your actions, but you will also create a culture of safety in your company. It will put your existing team at ease (allowing them to perform better at their job), and news of this culture will spread quickly so that soon your Glassdoor reviews will rise. This in turn will make your company a far more desirable place to work, and your rate of offer acceptance will go up dramatically.

Yes, doing the right thing often pays for itself several times over!

I call the process above "firing well." If you learn how to do it, then you also get the benefit of being able to let people go sooner, once you realize that they are not a fit, because doing so will not create trauma for the person, the company, or you. You can also take more chances on hiring people with high potential but less proven experience, since you now have a safe mechanism for ending the relationship if the potential doesn't materialize. These two actions will further strengthen your team and your company.

CHAPTER 30: **SALES AND MARKETING**

Sales and marketing are often grouped together because the goal of both is to get the product into customers' hands and money into the company's bank account. They are unique in their timing and processes, though. Salespeople directly interact with customers to identify if the product meets their needs and, if so, to close the sale. Marketing is the strategy that goes into identifying which customers most need the product and making sure they know about it.

I've invited sales expert Misha Talavera, co-founder of NeoReach, to share his expertise.

SALES

BY MISHA TALAVERA, CO-FOUNDER OF NEOREACH

In this section, I assume that you are selling a product and have found an initial version of product-market fit. I assume that you have successfully closed your initial paying customers, and these customers are satisfied enough with your product that a significant portion of them will become recurring customers. This section is divided into two parts: the first touches on the best practices for making a sale, and the second tackles how to build and manage a sales team and sales pipeline.

MAKING A SALE

To make a sale effectively, you need to do the following three things:

- Build trust
- Identify the customer's specific pain
- Sell results, not features

Build Trust

As in fundraising and recruiting, building trust is the primary goal, and it is achieved in the same way. For the first few meetings, try to only ask the potential customer about them, listen actively, reflect back what they say, and after each meeting, show that you remember what they said.

You may wonder how to get meetings in which you aren't required to talk about your product or service. Here are some ways:

- Be explicit about not talking about your company.
  - "Before we talk about what we do, I'd like to start by getting to know your situation, to know if we're even the right solution for you."
- Ask for a very limited amount of time so that the burden is low.
  - "Let's have a short introductory call for ten minutes."
  - "Let's get together for a quick coffee."
- Invite them to a purely social event.
  - "We're hosting drinks at ____ on ____. Please join us."
  - "We've got seats at the US Open. Please join us."

Identify the Customer's Specific Pain

To identify the customer's specific challenge, you must ask the right questions. This can be done either after you've built initial trust with the customer or as a way to build trust, since it involves listening to the customer. Either way, you need to understand your customer's pain before you present your solution.

By doing so you will achieve three things:

- You will know what the customer is looking for so you can present your solution in those same terms.
- The customer will know that your proposed solution is specifically intended to solve their specific challenge.

- You will weed out customers who aren't a good fit for your product and save time to focus on those who are.

So how do you do this? You ask a series of questions with the aim of understanding these three things:

- What are their goals?
- What are the challenges preventing them from reaching those goals?
- What are their ideal solutions to overcoming those obstacles?

As you will see in the following example, the conversation is not always as linear as you would hope. The pain point that you are solving may not be the only challenge that the customer faces, so it is your job to guide the conversation toward the specific pain you solve. It is also very helpful to ask open-ended questions, such as "Please tell me more." This will give you additional context about how they see the situation. Finally, make sure to repeat the important things they say about their goals, challenges, and ideal solutions back to them to show them that you are listening and to build trust. (Yes, this theme is never-ending.)

Me (preface): Hi, Stacey! It's good to have you on the phone. I'm looking forward to giving you a demo of NeoReach. Before I go ahead and do so, I would love to learn more about you and [company]. Can I ask you a couple of questions?

Stacey: Sure, that sounds good to me!

Me (goals): Awesome. So tell me, Stacey, what are you responsible for at [company]?

Stacey: I'm the director of social media, so I oversee our social media strategy across channels. This includes posting on our accounts, buying social ads, and working with social media influencers.

Me (goals): So you [repeat what she said]. Please tell me more about your influencer marketing.

Stacey: We mostly work with YouTube influencers, and they do product reviews for us. Last year, we worked with over four hundred influencers!

Me (goals): That's awesome. What are the goals of your influencer marketing, and how do you measure success?

Stacey: The goal of our influencer marketing is to build brand equity. We want to get the right influencers talking about our products to the right audiences. We measure success by measuring engagements.

Me (challenges): So [repeat what she said]. And what are your biggest obstacles or challenges with influencer marketing?

Stacey: My biggest obstacle right now is that I can't keep track of what my team is doing.

Me (challenges): [repeat what she said]. Please tell me more about that.

Stacey: My team uses spreadsheets to run the campaigns. As a result, it's really hard for me to know what each person is doing, how much we are spending, and the results that we're seeing.

Me (challenges): [repeat what she said]. Is that right?

Stacey: Yup.

Me (ideal solution): What would the ideal solution to your problem be?

Stacey: Ideally, I'd like to be able to easily see my team's activity, how much we are spending in any given month, and what results we are getting from each campaign and influencer.

Me (ideal solution): [repeat what she said]. And why is this important to you?

Stacey: Well, I really believe in influencer marketing, but unless I am able to get a clear view on our ROI, I cannot scale our spending.

Me: Got it! And please tell me, Stacey, how would a product like that be vetted and purchased at [company]?

Stacey: I'm the decision maker, but I would ask for the opinion of my influencer team and of my VP of marketing before pulling the trigger.

Me: Great. Well, Stacey, thank you so much for your answers. I would love to give you a demo of NeoReach. I think you may like what we've built for you.

Now that Stacey has clarified exactly what her pain point is, I feel confident that she will see value in our product, and I feel prepared to present my product in a way that addresses her top pain point.

As you do more of these calls, you will start to see trends. Your target customers will have many different related pain points that your product can solve, and different customers will highlight some over others. Taking notes is fundamental to record and categorize this knowledge.

Over time, you will want to build an inventory of problem and solution statements for the different kinds of customers and different product features your product serves. Here's an example:

Problem:

Directors of social media who oversee influencer marketing at Fortune 1000 consumer brands need a better way to track their influencer marketing activities, spending, and results.

Solution:

NeoReach is an influencer marketing SaaS platform that enables marketing managers to scale their influencer marketing by seamlessly tracking their influencer marketing activities, spending, and results, unlike spreadsheets, which are disorganized and scattered.

SELL RESULTS, NOT FEATURES

It's a classic founder issue to dive directly into the product functionality. After all, you've spent countless hours building this product, thinking through every feature and technical challenge. The reality, however, is that most people don't care about your product functionality. They don't care about your features. They care only about their business results.

Think about it: You don't buy the new MacBook because of its new chip. No, you buy the new MacBook because it allows you to achieve more due to its increased speed. It doesn't matter that it is faster because of the new chip. Heck, it could be faster because of some proprietary unicorn sparkle dust, and you would still buy it. What matters is that it helps you achieve more.

The chip is the how; achieving more is the why. Focus on the why. Focus on painting the vision of a world where the customer's desires are fulfilled with the help of your product.

Here's a real-world example. In the early days of DocuSign, the company was struggling to close big enterprise deals. They were selling software that enabled their customers' salespeople to send and sign contracts virtually. The problem was that nobody cared about signing contracts virtually. And why should they? There was no hint that signing contracts virtually had any impact on their bottom line.

When DocuSign realized this, they changed their strategy. They changed their pitch to say that they can increase your revenue by getting your customers to sign their contracts in under half the time that they currently take to do so. What follows is history. In 2015, DocuSign raised $233 million at a $3 billion valuation.

So what results are you providing to your target customers?

Beware the Dangers of Overselling

As a startup founder, you may be very tempted to be a yes-man to potential customers. After all, shouldn't you be trying to do everything possible to get revenue through the door?

As a result, many founders end up overselling, which leads to an inability to fully deliver. We do not recommend taking this route. Not only because it is ethically wrong—the customer trusts you to be honest about what you can and cannot do, and you are intentionally breaching that trust—but also because it has several quantifiable consequences for your business:

- Reputation: Customers talk to one another. There are only so many bridges you can burn before you burn your entire reputation in the market.
- Development team: Generally when founders oversell the product, they turn around and apply exorbitant pressure on the development team to meet the customer's oversold expectations. This can cause a lot of stress on the development team.
- Culture: Founders think it's okay to oversell because they are in control of the product. However, if the founders oversell, it is very likely that the sales hires will also oversell, since they will adopt the culture from the top. Once you create a culture of overselling, it is very hard to go back.

Overselling is a form of laziness. Instead, take the time to build trust. Then your customer will buy from you even though your product does not yet solve every one of their challenges. They trust that you will soon build in those features.

BUILDING A SALES TEAM AND PIPELINE

When should I hire a sales team? This is a common question among founders. Getting revenue in the door seems to be the solution to all your problems, and hiring salespeople seems to be the solution to getting revenue, so shouldn't you hire salespeople right now? The answer is no.

In most cases, salespeople will never be able to sell better than the founders, and they won't be able to sell the product if you are not able to. To thrive, salespeople need to have a very clear product offering to sell and very clear direction on whom to sell to. Furthermore, hiring salespeople will take up a lot of your headspace.

You should hire a sales team only when two conditions are met:

- You have found an initial version of product-market fit. This means that a significant proportion of your paying customers are renewing their contracts.
- You have figured out what you are selling and whom you are selling to.

Keep in mind that as you grow your sales, you also need to grow the infrastructure to meet the need of the sales from the new salespeople. This includes the onboarding process, customer support, and more.

THE STRUCTURE OF A SALES TEAM

(This section is based on Aaron Ross and Marylou Tyler's *Predictable Revenue*.)

Aaron Ross was an early hire at Salesforce.com. He is credited for designing the sales engine that grew Salesforce into a $100 million sales machine. Nowadays, his breakthroughs are implemented at all the winning B2B tech companies.

Aaron Ross's most important insight is this: Most executives think that the way to grow revenue is by adding salespeople. However, most often the main obstacle to growth is not growing the team but generating more leads. Only once you can predict your lead generation can you achieve predictable revenue. Only once you achieve predictable revenue can you achieve true scale.

Generating leads and closing deals are distinct functions that must be split. Generating leads is a game of breadth: it requires emailing and talking to a lot of different leads to filter out the non-qualified ones as fast as possible. Closing deals is a game of depth: it requires building deep relationships and understanding with the qualified leads in order to close the deal.

The people who close deals are often much more senior than the people who generate leads. This is because the relationship-building skill set often requires experience to develop.

Senior salespeople are expensive, so their time is best spent focusing on the most high-value activity: closing deals. If your salespeople are also generating leads, they are wasting valuable time and getting unnecessarily stressed by having to fulfill different functions in parallel.

Your customer success or account managers are the people who will tend to your existing customers, ensure their success, and grow the business coming from those customers. It's important to keep a good balance between generating new customers and tending to existing customers because it is very easy to get too focused on the former at the expense of the latter. Not only will great customer success make your customers happier and more likely to renew and increase their spending, but it will also give you an open channel of communication to the customer to receive feedback from them, which is the only way to continually improve your company and lead the market.

Here is the ideal structure of a sales team:

- Qualifiers (a.k.a. sales development reps): These people are focused on generating qualified leads and handing these off to the closers. Qualifiers are usually compensated with a base plus a bonus for each qualified lead they generate. Generally they are split into two groups:
  - Outbound reps: These are focused on proactively reaching out to leads and qualifying them. The most common channels used are email outreach and LinkedIn mining.
  - Inbound reps: These are focused on qualifying inbound leads that reach out to you by signing up to your site, signing up to your newsletter, or calling you directly.
- Closers (a.k.a. account executives, or AEs): These people are focused on closing the qualified leads generated for them by the qualifiers. Closers are compensated with a base plus a commission.
- Farmers (a.k.a. customer success): These people are focused on tending to existing customers, ensuring that these customers renew, and getting these customers to increase their spending. Farmers are compensated with a base plus a flat quarterly bonus based on retention rate or with a base plus a commission based on account growth.

Start hiring AEs only once you have a predictable flow of leads being generated and have farmers in place to tend to your customers. This means that you first want to hire a qualifier and a farmer while you act as the closer, and only once this system is running smoothly do you want to invest in an AE.

Common Mistakes in Hiring Salespeople

Here are some of the common mistakes made when hiring salespeople:

- Overlooking integrity and culture fit. Many people believe that the hiring rules that apply to the rest of their team don't apply to their sales team because salespeople are heartless mercenaries.

As a result, they end up hiring salespeople who are that way, and this becomes a self-fulfilling prophecy. It is true that salespeople are generally more motivated by money than product people. However, that does not diminish the importance of hiring salespeople with integrity, culture fit, and mission alignment. They exist, it's just a matter of looking for them.

- Not investing in training. Despite their track record at other companies, if your salespeople don't know about your industry, your product, and your process, they will not be operating at max capacity. The best sales teams put their new recruits through an intensive training program, which includes working with the product, customer success, and sales development teams.
- Hiring only senior AEs with a track record. Many of the best sales teams are built from young, previously inexperienced closers. While track record is important, having the sales DNA (relationship-building skills), attention to process, and commitment to the company vision often have more impact on salespeople's performance.
- Hiring a solo contributor (AE) rather than a manager (VP of sales). Contrary to popular belief, the best closers are most often not the best managers. This is because there is practically no overlap between the skill set required to run a team and manage a sales pipeline and those required for closing individual deals. When hiring a VP of sales, don't fall into the trap of hiring the best solo performer. Rather, the best way is to hire a sales manager with a proven track record of management.

Lead Generation

Generating predictable leads is the first step to achieving predictable revenue. Not all leads are generated in the same way, so not all leads have the same needs. Specifically there are three kinds of leads:

- **Seeds:** Seeds are generated from word of mouth, usually from customer referrals or prior relationships.

- Pros: They tend to close fast, have high win rates, and grow into your best customers.
- Cons: It is really hard to proactively grow them; the best thing you can do is build an awesome product and customer success team.
- **Nets:** Nets are generated from your marketing, such as events, SEO, white papers, and ad campaigns. They are called nets because you are going for quantity over quality. Your inbound reps will then qualify the leads.
  - Pros: If done well, they can be very scalable and cost-effective.
  - Cons: There are serious costs and time associated with building, optimizing, and maintaining this channel.
- **Spears:** Spears are generated from direct outbound outreach by your outbound reps, usually through email outreach or LinkedIn mining. They are called spears because they are hypertargeted and you are going for quality over quantity.
  - Pros: They are predictable, hypertargeted, and deliver immediate results.
  - Cons: They require having full-time outbound reps and may not be profitable if your average annual deal size is under $10,000.

Unless your deal sizes are very small (in which case spears may be unprofitable for you), the three types of leads are very complementary and should be given attention. For instance, some of the leads you generate may not be ready to buy, so your email marketing (a net strategy) can nurture those leads until they are ready.

Generally startups get their first customers from seeds: referrals from friends, investors, and other customers. As you start to scale, it is recommended to focus next on spears. This is because spears generate hypertargeted leads and immediate results, while nets generate a broader set of leads and take time to set up. That being said, each industry, target customer, and product has different needs. It is your job to figure out what channels deliver the best results and narrow in on those.

If you are scaling up your spears strategy, I recommend that you use an outsourced third party to identify lead emails for you based on your target customer profile. Your outbound reps can then use a platform like Reply.io to send drip email campaigns and generate leads more effectively.

Qualifying Leads and Handoff

The main focus of your qualifiers (outbound and inbound reps) is to qualify leads and pass those off to the AEs to close. The best practice here is to create a qualification checklist that your qualifiers will be responsible for checking off. Often this is done by scheduling a call with the prospect and going through the checklist.

Every company has their own specific qualification checklist. Generally, a qualified lead is one that

- feels the pain point that your product is solving,
- has the desire to solve that pain point, and
- has the power to purchase your product.

Once the qualifier has qualified the lead, they must pass it off to the AE. This is best done by introducing the AE in the email thread with the prospect or by having the AE join the next call with the prospect.

Qualifiers should be compensated either on a flat fee for each qualified lead they generate or on a percentage of the deals that they generate that are closed by the AE. For this reason, it is imperative that the AE be the one who decides if a lead is actually qualified. Generally the AE is the one who marks the lead as qualified in the CRM, not the qualifier.

Sales KPIs

While there is an art to building relationships, scaling a sales engine is a science that can be optimized and predicted. In order to do so, you and your team must be rigorous about your KPIs and process.

Let's start with KPIs. The metrics you choose to track are the metrics you will optimize around, so choose them wisely.

Here are some of the main KPIs I recommend that you track:

- Average deal size: Average dollar amount per customer
- New revenue per month: Total new revenue closed in a given month; can be split between what channel it came from and whether it came from an existing customer or a new customer
- Average sales cycle length: Average time it takes from when a lead is qualified to when it is closed
- Number of SQLs per month: Number of qualified leads passed off to AEs per month
- Cost per lead: Average cost per qualified lead passed off to AEs
- Customer acquisition cost: The total cost of acquiring a new customer, including marketing costs and salaries
- Customer churn rate: Percentage of customers who don't renew in any given month
- Revenue churn rate: Percentage of revenue that doesn't renew in any given month

Remember to create countermetrics as well.

CRM platforms can help you streamline your sales process and KPI tracking. Salesforce is the leader in the space, and I recommend using that platform once you have over ten full-time salespeople. Until then, I recommend that you pick a lighter-weight CRM to save time on the setup. I recommend SalesforceIQ.

MARKETING: SEGMENT, TARGET, PROMOTE

Marketing can be defined as understanding the problems of customers (strategic marketing) and what solutions are offered in the marketplace (competitive analysis), creating a solution that more effectively solves the customer problem (product management), and letting customers know that your solution exists (tactical marketing).

The essential goal of strategic marketing and competitive analysis is choosing your target beachhead. The essential goal of product management is achieving product-market fit. And the essential goal of tactical marketing is growing sales.

Let's say you have discovered a way to disrupt a massive legacy market. You are the first to go after this opportunity, and you want to get as many customers as you can, as fast as you can. Your first instinct is to reach out to any and all potential customers in the space. You may even have the thought that you want a few customers in each geographical area around the world to mark your territory. Your primary fear is that other competitors will see the same opportunity and move faster than you.

But history tells a different story. The greatest risk of a startup is not that they moved too slowly in dominating the entire marketplace, but rather that they spread their scarce resources too thin and ended up securing few or no customers at all.

Every customer already has a legacy solution in place, and those legacy providers are far larger with more resources than you. They have deep and long-standing relationships with their customers. Even if your product or service is better, it needs to be ten times better than the legacy solution for a customer to switch.

Therefore, rather than go after the entire market at once, the key is to find a small segment of the market (i.e., a set of customers with similar pain points) that has a particularly difficult problem for whom your solution is indeed ten times better than the broad, nonspecific legacy solution. This is your low-hanging fruit. Concentrate all your efforts on this type of customer to maximize your chance of getting your first few customers. Once you do, you will then have a track record to share, be able to raise more money, and be able to hire more engineers to create more features and more salespeople to develop more relationships. Continue focusing on this first type of customer until you have secured many (if not most) of them as your customers. Then use your now-larger amount of resources to move to the next-lowest-hanging fruit.

A good analogy is the Allied invasion of Europe during World War II. The Germans held the whole coastline. The Allies could have chosen to spread their invading force along the entire shore. If they had, they would have had one boat per beach. The Germans pillboxes would have slaughtered each and every Allied soldier who landed on a French beach.

That, of course, is not what the Allies did. Instead, they studied the coastline and found the beach that was the least well defended (Normandy). They concentrated all their forces on that one target beachhead and so were able to overwhelm the German defenses there and secure the toehold they needed. From there, the Allies were able to bring in more resources, expand out, and eventually spread throughout Europe.

Do the same. Study the marketplace. Segment it into different customer types. Determine which segment is the least satisfied with their current solution and for whom your solution is the best fit. Concentrate all your sales and engineering efforts toward this segment. Land a few of these customers. Continue to focus on this segment until you dominate it. Only then expand to other customer segments (or add other products).

The best way to choose a target beachhead is to follow the steps outlined in the book *Disciplined Entrepreneurship* by Bill Aulet. There is no need to reinvent the wheel here; that book outlines the steps clearly.

CONCLUSION: **MAKE MONEY, HAVE FUN, DO GOOD**

This book is intended to give you the roadmap to turn your company into a massive financial success. If it does, treat yourself: Go have fun, and lots of it. Until you don't want to have fun anymore. And when that moment arrives, I ask that you take one more step: do good in the world. By this, I don't mean write checks to pleasant-sounding charities. I mean get your hands dirty. You already know how to do this. When you first started your company, you discovered your customers' pains and then figured out the least costly and most scalable solutions to those pain points. Now do it again, but this time with the least noticed people in your community (likely the poorest and most marginalized). There will be no financial payoff if you do. You likely will get no praise or thanks. But you will have made a truly positive contribution to the world. And you will know it. When you do, you will experience the rarest and most exquisite of feelings: the satisfaction of a life well lived. That is the true gift that I want to give you!

ACKNOWLEDGMENTS

This book could not have happened without all the people whom I have coached, and who coach me, including Chris Barber, Misha Talavera, Ryan Breslow, Alex MacCaw, Naval Ravikant, Brian Armstrong, Tatiana Dorow, Alexander Kasser, and Stephen and Mary Mochary.

We each had to put in so much to make this book happen. Chris Barber "found" me and invited me to coach his roommates at Stanford, which launched my coaching career. Misha, Ryan, and Alex, all of whom I coached, forced me to get these writings into the world: Misha by writing the sections that I wasn't motivated to, Ryan by pushing me when I stalled, and Alex by finally just tweeting it out (after asking my permission, of course). Naval read an early draft and said it was the best business book he'd seen (whether true or not, that's what he told me), further encouraging me to get it out into the world. Brian also read an early draft and, based on that, asked me to coach him. My wife, Tatiana, well, she just makes my life great by making me laugh each and every day. Alexander, my grandfather, made me feel that I could never fail, no matter how hard I swung the bat. Stephen and Mary, my parents, have always been my biggest fans.

Writing this book was most difficult for me when it was almost done. I very much enjoyed writing the content. But the final stages of editing and formatting felt like work. Luckily, Alex pushed me through those tasks.

As a group, we were driven by our vision of sharing this information with the world so that CEOs and companies could be more efficient and effective.

I am so proud and thankful that I got a chance to work with this amazing group of people. All the people I coach will likely say that I have added value to their lives. I hope they realize that they have fundamentally transformed mine into one of never-ending joy. (Yes, I appreciate them often, so I'm pretty sure that they know.)

My wish for you is that one day you too get the chance to experience the joy of coaching others. It is the most deeply satisfying activity that I have yet found in life. If you know of anything more satisfying, please tell me!

APPENDIX: TO IPO, OR NOT TO IPO?

To IPO, or not to IPO? That is the question.

When your company is doing well, there are many people who will want you to take the company public: investors, employees, advisers, friends, family, and so on. Publicly traded shares create the most liquidity at (usually) the highest price for investors and employees alike. The company's lawyers, bankers, and accountants make tremendous fees at the IPO and upon subsequent transactions. Friends and family members take pride in your company being publicly traded.

With all these incentives in place, an IPO may feel like a forgone conclusion. *It's not!*

Publicly traded shares do give a company financial flexibility. But they remove operational flexibility. There is a pernicious cascade of unintended consequences that gets put in place upon an IPO that lead to a set of virtual shackles being placed on your (and your company's) ankles and wrists.

Here's how it works:

The strength of your company's equity value allows you to retain great team members and acquire accretive companies. If your stock value drops significantly and for a sustained period, many of your best people will leave. (Their options value will have dried up, and they have the ability to get hired elsewhere.) Likewise, acquisitions will become too expensive to make. These dynamics will negatively and materially impact your ability to run the company well. Therefore, you will do whatever you can to make sure that the stock price does not drop significantly. And this is where the cascade begins.

Each quarter, you will have to both project next quarter's performance and report on last quarter's actuals. There will be pressure to project growth each and every quarter. If not, shareholders will sell. Once projected, there will be even greater pressure to meet or exceed these projections. If not, shareholders will sell. The hamster wheel has begun to spin.

Now enter the short sellers who believe that you will at some point fall off this hamster wheel. They take a short position in your stock, and suddenly their incentive is to show the world all the worst things about your company so that the stock price drops now. Some of these short sellers have integrity, and some don't. Those who don't are willing to spread rumors, lies, and innuendo. While they may be dealing in fiction, the consequences for you are very real.

And finally there are the very real costs of satisfying the SEC's reporting requirements (Sarbanes-Oxley). This likely costs several million dollars a year in accounting and legal fees. But even more costly is the significant management overhead involved.

These days, the private markets offer tremendous amounts of capital (e.g., SoftBank, sovereign wealth funds, Tiger Global Management, Coatue, GV) at strong valuations. Before choosing to create public equity, reach out to public company CEOs and ask them what the cost/benefit really is.

Mark Zuckerberg wanted to keep Facebook private forever. But because many of his employees were exercising their options and selling on the secondary market to create liquidity, the company was at risk of exceeding five hundred "owners." At this threshold, the SEC requires that a company have publicly traded shares. In order not to run afoul of the law, Facebook went public.

Having seen this example, Palantir partnered with a secondary fund to offer liquidity to its employees so that they would never trip the five-hundred-plus owner barrier.

Instead of giving in to all the voices around you (particularly from your institutional venture investors) who want you to go public, consider staying private. Capital is abundant in this world. Operational freedom, once lost, is very difficult to regain.

ESSENTIAL READING

The problems encountered in starting, growing, and running a company have been faced by thousands of CEOs before. And luckily dozens of successful CEOs and business leaders have written down their lessons learned. These books teach us almost every important aspect of running a business. While there are hundreds of such books, the following are my favorites, and I consider them required reading for any CEO or manager. Please do read them at some point soon.

INDIVIDUAL PRODUCTIVITY

Getting Things Done: The Art of Stress-Free Productivity
David Allen
10 hours reading time
Personal productivity; describes using pen and paper, but I recommend translating that method to Evernote or another electronic tool. Using this system will make you sleep better. It takes several days to fully implement the system, but the time investment is very much worth it.

ORGANIZATIONAL PRODUCTIVITY

The One Minute Manager
Kenneth Blanchard and Spencer Johnson
0.5 hours
Simple reporting structure that works. Simple enough that you can have all your team members read it. I recommend that you do. (Some of it is obviously dated. Ignore those parts.)

High Output Management
Andrew S. Grove
10 hours

The classic tech management book. A lot more detail than *The One Minute Manager*, but essentially the same structure.

The Hard Thing about Hard Things: Building a Business When There Are No Easy Answers
Ben Horowitz
6 hours
Says how great *High Output Management* is, and then talks about what to do in some very specific and ugly situations that no other books discuss.

SALES AND MARKETING

Disciplined Entrepreneurship: 24 Steps to a Successful Startup
Bill Aulet
12 hours
A painful but very necessary step-by-step guide to determining who your real customer is, what solution they want, and how to market and sell to them. If you read and apply only one of these books, make it this one.

Never Split the Difference: Negotiating as If Your Life Depended on It
Chris Voss
6 hours
Ostensibly about negotiation, but really about how to create deep connection and trust quickly, which is the key to an excellent relationship with your three key constituents: customers (sales), employees (management), and investors (fundraising). This is the best book on sales that I have found.

RECRUITING

Who
Geoff Smart and Randy Street
6 hours
Excellent recruiting process that maximizes the likelihood of hiring only A players and then ensuring their success at the company.

CULTURE

The 15 Commitments of Conscious Leadership: A New Paradigm for Sustainable Success
Jim Dethmer, Diana Chapman, and Kaley Warner Klemp
10 hours
Companies can become good using the hard skills outlined in the books
   above. To become great, a company must become curious and open
   to learning. This books shows how to do that.

ADDITIONAL READING

The 7 Habits of Highly Effective People: Powerful Lessons in Personal Change
Stephen Covey

"How to Become Insanely Well-Connected"
First Round Review
https://firstround.com/review/how-to-become-insanely-well-connected/

"Why You Need Two Chiefs in the Executive Office"
First Round Review
https://firstround.com/review/why-you-need-two-chiefs-in-the-executive
   -office/

13 Days: A Memoir of the Cuban Missile Crisis
Robert F. Kennedy

"Don't Drown in Email! How to Use Gmail More Efficiently"
Andreas Klinger
https://klinger.io/post/71640845938/dont-drown-in-email-how-to
   -use-gmail-more

Essentialism: The Disciplined Pursuit of Less
Greg McKeown

"What Is Founder-Friendly Stock and Should I Use It in My Startup?"
Jeron Paul
https://www.capshare.com/blog/what-is-founderfriendly-stock-and
-should-i-use-it-in-my-startup/

Nonviolent Communication: A Language of Life
Marshall B. Rosenberg

Predictable Revenue: Turn Your Business into a Sales Machine with the $100 Million Best Practices of Salesforce.com
Aaron Ross and Marylou Tyler

Unconventional Success: A Fundamental Approach to Personal Investment
David F. Swensen

"All Hail, Emperor Zuckerberg: How Facebook's IPO Gives a Stunning and Unprecedented Amount of Power to Its CEO"
Matthew Yglesias
https://slate.com/business/2012/02/facebooks-ipo-how-mark-zuckerberg
-plans-to-retain-dictatorial-control-his-company.html

ABOUT THE AUTHOR

Matt Mochary coaches Silicon Valley tech CEOs and heads of tech investment firms on how to be the best leaders and build the best organizations possible. Matt shows CEOs how to perform the role by modeling it: he has been a "one-day-a-week CEO" at Brex, Clearbit, OpenAI, AngelList, and Bolt.

Matt graduated from Yale University with a BA in humanities and the Kellogg School of Management with an MBA. He began his business career as an investor with Spectrum Equity in Menlo Park. He then co-founded Totality, which was eventually sold to MCI/Verizon and is now called Verizon Business. Matt went on to have fun (making the documentary *Favela Rising*, which was short-listed for an Academy Award) and do good (starting the Mochary Foundation).

When I joined Spectrum Equity after business school, many friends and friends of friends began reaching out to me for career advice. The ploy was a thin one. They really wanted a job at Spectrum. There was no such job available to them, but I earnestly gave them career advice. They each said that they wanted a job where they could "make money, have fun, and do good." I replied, "Great, but if you had to choose just one of those, which would it be?" The answer was inevitably "Make money." I then told them to optimize only for that variable. If they tried to optimize for all three, they'd end up in a place that provided none.

After giving this advice over and over, I realized that I needed to follow it myself. So I started my own company and, eighteen months later, was lucky enough to have amassed more wealth than I knew what to do with.

Having checked the box of "make money," I turned my attention to "have fun." I made it my full-time job. And I became very good at it. I did it for three years straight, until I had so much fun that I was over it.

Now what? Well, "do good" seemed the next logical step. And, to me, this didn't mean give money to charities. It meant doing the really dirty work: helping people others were afraid to help. To me, that meant helping hardcore criminals in the United States. And that's when I decided to set up the Mochary Foundation.

If you're looking for an important problem to address, here is one: Millions of formerly incarcerated Americans struggle to get jobs because every employer can easily do a background check, and the vast majority of employers will not hire someone with a criminal record if there is another candidate available. That leaves formerly incarcerated people with almost no way of making legitimate money. But they still need to eat. So they do whatever they have to in order to eat. And this often leads them right back to prison.

The solution, in my opinion, is a short vocational training program for high-skill jobs for which there is a shortage of qualified candidates. The Mochary Foundation trains ex-convicts to get their commercial driver's license. Within days of getting their license, they are usually driving a truck for over $50,000 a year, and suddenly their future seems stable and tenable. Trucking companies are so desperate for drivers that they are willing to pay recruiter fees that more than pay for the cost of training the driver. Thus, this operation can be self-funding.

The Mochary Foundation is now starting to scale this solution. But we have zero pride in ownership. In fact, we would love for lots of people, companies, and governments to steal the ideas and processes. We want the solution to spread, but we don't need to be the ones to do it.

So if you or your entity wants to do this work and you want our blueprint, please reach out to the Mochary Foundation. We'll gladly hand you all our secrets!

CPSIA information can be obtained
at www.ICGtesting.com
Printed in the USA
BVHW010935160921
616786BV00017B/68